The Essential
Guide to
Child
Obesity

SERIES EDITOR

Published in Great Britain in 2018 by
need2know
Remus House
Coltsfoot Drive
Peterborough
PE2 9BF
Telephone 01733 898103
www.need2knowbooks.co.uk

Contents

Introduction

Hi there! This book is for parents, grandparents, guardians and carers of children ranging from toddlers to teenagers. If you've picked up this book to learn about the healthy weight for a child in your life, you've come to the right place. Professional childcare workers, educators and anyone interested in children's health may also find this book valuable. Obesity rates in the UK have been rising at an alarming rate; obesity in children has more than trebled in the past 20 years with 10% of six-year-olds and 20% of all ten-year-olds now classified as obese.

The topic is rarely out of the news these days and much of the information is alarming. Also, younger and younger children are now picking up on body image and becoming confused a lot earlier in their lives about what represents a healthy size and weight. Our goal is to lay out simply and easily all the facts you need to know about obesity and other weight problems, and how a child and their guardian might work together to tackle it. It's not a disease that strikes at random; it's a condition that can occur because of particular circumstances and can be very successfully treated and prevented from recurring. This is a problem we need to deal with right now, as experts[1] have estimated that by the year 2050, 50% of females and 60% of males will be obese if we continue on our current trajectory.

Tackling child obesity early helps children lay the foundation stone for a healthy life. Many parents are growing concerned about their children's health, and want to know the facts about how these headlines and statistics will really affect them. A lot of support is available out there for parents, thanks to the massive awareness brought to the subject by its high profile in the media.

Although this book often refers to "your child", it is intended as a resource for anyone concerned with children's welfare, whether they are relatives, friends, teachers, childcare workers or professionals. Whatever your situation, you can guarantee you won't be the only person seeking help on this subject: childhood obesity and weight issues are very common, and the average UK class can contain as many as three or four children with the condition.

You'll be able to help yourself and your entire family when you help your child, by putting in place an active, balanced life that the whole family can enjoy. This book is to be used as a reference guide or handbook to childhood obesity, and should not be used as a replacement for professional advice.

---

1   Lobstein T, Leach RJ. Foresight tackling obesities: future choices international comparisons of obesity trends, determinants and responses—evidence review. 2007.

A Note to the Reader

The upshot is that around 3-4 children in a typical class of 30 will now be obese and many more of those will be overweight. Family breakdown, chaotic lifestyles, busy working lives, the easy availability of junk food and the growth of technology have all changed the way we live. When we initially started researching this subject, it quickly became obviously how much the life of the average child has changed over the last few decades, and just how easy it is for unhealthy habits to make their way into your life.

All these changes mean that many children consume far more calories and unhealthy foods than they used to, while being a lot less active than they would have been just 10 years ago. Tam Fry of the National Obesity Forum believes the best way to tackle child obesity is prevention, not intervention. They explain that "we need to start looking at the national curriculum and getting cooking back on the menu for children, as well as offering help to pregnant women as part of their ante-natal screening."

Tam Fry says that some families are getting the message and taking steps to help themselves but they tend to be better off than others who can't or won't start to make the difficult changes which will give results. With this in mind, we have streamlined the advice in this book and included a wider range of links relevant to people all over the UK, including black and minority ethnic children as there are special factors affecting these groups.

For a number of years, there have been constant outcries in the media about obesity rates, but there hasn't been that much improvement in that time. Fry continues, "it's much easier and cheaper to stop children becoming overweight than it is to try and get adults to lose weight, but at the moment, there isn't enough being done to make a big difference." If we aren't able to catch children at a young age, it can be very difficult to tackle the consequences that appear as they grow up.

It's important that we keep in mind that while the situation may seem dire, there's plenty of support and guidance out there to help the carers and guardians of children with weight issues.

Disclaimer

Professional medical advice should not be replaced by the information in this book, which is intended to provide only general information on childhood obesity and weight issues. This book may be used alongside professional medical advice, but those planning to change their child's lifestyle should first consult a doctor or other healthcare professional.

What Are We Talking About?

Overweight? Obese? What do we mean?

Considering that Foresight, a government sponsored project, has predicted that by 2050 a quarter of all Britain's children will be obese, it's in the interests of every parent to make sure that their child is not storing up problems for the future. A lot of people are happy to throw around the term "obese" without fully understanding what it means. Obesity is a precise medical term which a doctor can arrive at by measuring a patient's BMI (Body Mass Index).

This is is a process which involves comparing the patient's height and weight and dividing weight (in kilogrammes) by height (in metres) squared. Obesity in adults is defined by a BMI of over 30. The clinical definition of being overweight and obese for children is based on growth charts known as centile charts, with different ones for boys and girls. The best ways to measure and define child obesity are still under debate, as children are constantly growing and changing and adult calculations are unable to allow for this.

Centile charts allow weights to be plotted with different cut-off points depending on a child's age and height. We'll talk about this in greater detail later in the book. Action needs to be taken by parents as early as possible, so there's no need to wait for a doctor to officially label your child "obese" before introducing healthier lifestyle components. Make sure you are not storing up problems for the future: if your child's weight is causing them difficulties, affecting their participation in normal childhood activities or their self-confidence, it's time to take action.

A Weighty Problem

The topic is never out of the media, and despite all of this interest, obesity rates are still on the rise and we're still heading for a fat future. Weight and obesity aren't just a concern for parents. The child obesity epidemic is becoming a major issue for educators, the NHS and the government. And between constant discussion of crash diets and coverage of celebrity body shapes, the media attention isn't helping all that much.

Just imagine how a child must feel when faced with a barrage of contradictions about body shape and size – it's no wonder children are starting to starve and stuff themselves at increasingly young ages. What's a parent to do?

Effects on Mental Health

Usually, emotional and psychological problems are the first to occur in obese children. Peers of obese children will often bully them, and sometimes discrimination and harassment will even take place in their own families. Low self-esteem and depression can easily develop as a result of the negative stereotypes these children are forced to deal with.

Pop Quiz!

We'll get down to the serious stuff soon but first, why not give our fun quiz a go to see how much you know about healthy eating and exercise?

Low self-esteem and depression can easily develop as a result of the negative stereotypes these children are forced to deal with.

	Question 1: What does a normal Sunday afternoon look like for your family?	
A	Chilling out/Surfing the web with snack and drink in hand/ Sitting in front of a screen watching TV.	☐
B	We thought about going to the pool but it was too cold so we stayed at home and had a pyjama day.	☐
C	We ate lunch as a family after the kids' sports classes, then went for a family bike ride.	☐

	Question 2: How do mealtimes work in your house?	
A	Everyone chooses their own favourite foods to eat, then we all sit in front of the TV to eat.	☐
B	We cook healthy dinners, but the kids don't like vegetables so we give them chicken nuggets and chips to keep the peace.	☐
C	We sit down to three meals a day as a family, and the children help to prepare, serve and tidy away afterwards.	☐

	Question 3: How often do you walk to or from school with your children.	
A	Never – We have two cars and no time to walk as we're on our way to work.	☐
B	We've done it a couple of times but it's difficult to organise and almost nobody else does it.	☐
C	We leave the car at home unless the weather is terrible or we really can't do without it.	☐

	Question 4: How often do your kids actually eat five pieces of fruit or veg in a day?	
A	Never – They don't like fruit and vegetables and won't eat them.	☐
B	I give them an apple in their lunch box and there's always fruit at home.	☐
C	We make sure fresh fruit and vegetables are served with every meal and are given as snacks.	☐

	Question 5: How often do you eat fast food or takeaways?	
A	At least 3 or 4 times each week – It's the kids' favourite food.	☐
B	We try to limit ourselves to once a week but they enjoy this type of food and sometimes it's just very convenient.	☐
C	We have them on special occasions, but as a general rule we try to avoid fast food.	☐

	Question 6: What goes in your child's lunch box?	
A	White bread sandwich, processed cheese stick, a can of fizzy drink and some snacks like chocolate, crisps or sweets.	☐
B	Cheese sandwich on white bread (my child won't eat brown bread), crisps, an apple, some biscuits and a juice carton.	☐
C	Water, Greek salad, fruit salad, wholemeal pitta bread with cottage cheese and cucumber, dried fruit, grissini and a low fat, reduced sugar yoghurt.	☐

	Question 7: How physically active is your family?	
A	Sport is really important in our family: We watch every match and buy all the latest Fifa games, which the kids play all the time.	☐
B	We love to watch football and rugby but my son never gets picked for the team and my teenage daughter doesn't like school sports.	☐
C	We encourage our kids to join as many teams and clubs as possible, and go swimming every weekend.	☐

	Question 8: Which best describes your weekly shop?	
A	Supermarket sweep: our trolley is filled with as many snacks and treats for the kids as we can fit! Special offers determine most of our purchases. Why get one litre of cola when we could get two?	☐
B	We try to be good and stick to our list but those special offers are very tempting and the kids slip stuff into the trolley.	☐
C	We follow our list, and always make time to read ingredients and search for low-fat alternatives. We try not to buy tempting things like snacks and treats.	☐

	Question 9: If you drive to school, where do you park?	
A	As close to the school gate as possible so we don't have too far to walk. If there are no wardens about, I'll leave the car on double yellow lines.	☐
B	We don't try too hard to park right in front of the school, but the kids will complain if they have to walk too far.	☐
C	On the rare occasions we take the car, we'll park around the corner and enjoy the walk to school.	☐

	Question 10: It's lunchtime and you have places to be. What's on the menu?	
A	Head to the Drive-Thru! That's the cheapest way to get filling food in a rush.	☐
B	We'll tide ourselves over with some crisps or biscuits. We can always get another snack later if we're still hungry.	☐
C	I knew this would happen, so I made a salad earlier today. All that's left to do is eat!	☐

How did you do?

Mostly As

It's great that you've taken the time to answer this quiz honestly! There are a few changes you'll need to make in your household when it comes to your children's health, and hopefully some of those will be clear to you after that quiz. If your children aren't overweight, it's very likely they will be soon enough.

Mostly Bs

You seem to have some ideas about how to keep your kids happy and healthy, but you don't quite know how to put those plans into action. Try to focus on making some changes that fit in with your lifestyle, rather than just thinking about all the things you can't do right now. Try to set a good example for your children by making changes in your own life.

Mostly Cs

You're no stranger to a healthy lifestyle, that's for sure! It sounds like you have things more or less in control so far. Just make sure you continue on the trajectory you're on right now, and you'll be fine!

All in the name of fun!

It should be obvious what the best choices are here – this quiz is really just meant to be a bit of fun. It's pretty unlikely that you're making as many bad decisions as Family A, or that you're quite as strict as Family C. Most people are somewhere in the middle, and want to give their children a healthier life but don't know where to begin.

It's no fun to be a seriously overweight child who isn't able to make the necessary decisions to change. If you take anything away from this quiz, it should be that it's a parent's responsibility to make the right choice for their children.

Children's Weight: What Are the Facts?

There are 10 facts that everyone needs to know about obesity, according to the World Health Organisation.

1 In the UK, obesity has become an epidemic.

2 If you don't burn off all the calories you eat, this can eventually lead to obesity.

3 Children from certain ethnic groups and deprived communities tend to be more prone to obesity.

4 In the last few decades, our eating habits have changed a lot.

5 Increased physical activity and healthy eating are the best way to combat obesity.

6 There is a lot of support for people who need help in combating obesity.

7 Most children and adults are not active enough.

8 Nobody is responsible for being overweight or obese.

9 The cost of obesity to society is enormous.

10 Children especially are in danger of becoming obese.

To see how these facts apply to our children, it's worth looking at them in detail.

1. The Obesity "Epidemic"

Any disease, condition or illness that occurs on a much larger scale than normal and affects many more people than expected can be referred to as an epidemic. In 2002, one in 20 boys and one in 15 girls aged 2-15 were obese. This high occurrence of obesity may help children to understand that they are far from unique and there are many others in the same situation.

The rising numbers of overweight and obese children have been tracked by the charity Weight Concern. At present, two thirds of adults, a quarter of 2-10 year olds and one third of 11-15 year olds are overweight or obese. It's been estimated that if trends like these continue, 70% of all adults will be overweight or obese by the year 2034.

2. Always burn off what you eat

This seems to be the message that people have the most difficulty with, even though it's one of the simplest ideas out there! Teaching this to children will give them something to focus on. If they can get an understanding of the link between calories and activity, it's a great way to illustrate the issue.

3. Obesity is linked to social deprivation and ethnic background

If you look at the statistics on a map, you will see that there tend to be more cases of obesity in inner city areas. Less well-off areas tend to house higher concentrations of obesity, according to the latest Scottish and English health surveys. A vicious circle can appear in the lives of many children, where they become obese because of social inequalities, and are then discriminated against further as a result of obesity.

Data from the National Child Measurement Programme (NCMP) that has been running in England since 2006, found that in reception classes (aged 4-5 years) obesity prevalence is especially high for children from Black African and Black ethnic groups, and boys from the Bangladeshi ethnic group. An analysis of trends in obesity prevalence by ethnic groups using NCMP statistics found a trend of rising obesity for both boys and girls of Bangladeshi ethnicity.

Adolescents from minority ethnic groups were also less likely to be switched on to healthy eating and more likely to adopt junk food diets. A review of what children from BME groups eat, found children from South Asian ethnic groups, and most notably Bangladeshi children, have a higher overall energy intake. Children from Black African and Black Caribbean backgrounds were found to have a lower intake of fat.

Concern has been growing in recent years about children from black and minority ethnic groups. According to one NHS report, "In terms of public health action, it is particularly important for South Asian populations in the UK to be aware of the health risks of increased BMI and waist circumference." (Obesity and Ethnicity, NHS report by the National Obesity Observatory, January 2011).

South Asian children also appear to be less active – the Child Heart and Health Study in England (CHASE) reported lower physical activity levels in British South Asian children compared to White European, Black African or Black Caribbean children, with girls

Adolescents from minority ethnic groups were also less likely to be switched on to healthy eating and more likely to adopt junk food diets.

less active than boys. There is also a strong link between obesity and the surroundings people live in with more ethnic minorities living in built-up areas surrounded by fast food takeaways.

Certain sections of the BME community share the same problem, even though the acronym is used to describe a wide range of communities, faiths and cultures. Studies have also suggested that certain Asian groups, such as children from Pakistani and Bangladeshi backgrounds, have a higher rate of obesity than those from Black ethnic and Black African backgrounds.

Other studies have suggested that the estimations of obesity and obesity-related illnesses among these minority ethnic groups may be under-reported, and that the rates may be greatly increased if revised measurements were used. White girls, according to the HABITS survey, experience a more gradual drop in physical activity than girls from Asian backgrounds.

Children of ethnic minority groups found that their physical activities were influenced greatly by a lack of facilities in which to exercise combined with worries about their safety.

4. In the last few decades, our eating habits have changed a lot.

Portion sizes have grown as food has become cheaper and children's spending power means that for a few pounds they can buy much bigger bars of chocolate and packets of sweets. We have a vast and tempting choice of different types of food every time we visit one of our well-stocked supermarkets. Everything from technology to cultural attitudes has shifted greatly in recent years, and our diet is no different.

Children are tempted by lots of brands and foods aimed at them specifically and it can be very difficult to resist pester power. By now, we don't even need to spend any energy cooking for our families as many of our meals come pre-prepared. Some burger meals can contain a child's entire caloric needs for the whole day, with take-outs, high energy drinks, ready meals and processed foods more calorie-packed than ever before.

The current combination of too much of the wrong type of food and not enough exercise is a recipe for disaster, however wonderful it is to have a big range of foods to choose from and greater opportunities to shop. Just remember that with great spending power comes great consumption responsibility.

5. Eat well and stay active!

If your child understands how important these two elements are, they will be on the way to success. Success in combating obesity will only come if you and your family combine a healthy diet with an active lifestyle. Schools, the health service, local councils and supermarkets all have an important role to play in ensuring they keep our children healthy by providing healthy food choices and opportunities to become more active.

Making sure that these two things are done is not just your child's responsibility, and it's important we all remember that. Better quality foods, according to experts from the World Health Organisation, need to replace the energy-dense drinks and snacks that fill our children's diets, and healthy food options need to be made more affordable and widely available in school canteens and shops.

This action must be backed by the authorities and everyone involved in the food industry, local government and educational and sporting industries. The WHO also suggest that workplace programmes and schools should provide opportunities for everyday physical activities.

6. There is a lot of support for people who need help in combating obesity.

Once you find out what help, support and information is available, it should be much easier to make progress. All the countries in Europe have made a commitment to work towards improving child obesity through increased exercise and healthy food choices. Efforts to combat the obesity epidemic are being taken by schools, members of the food industry, supermarkets, the health service and the government, which is great news for parents and children alike.

Community information, help and support are all available from a wide range of resources. Unless you ask, however, these resources won't just be handed to you. You'll need to look for them and request them yourself. We'll talk about this in greater detail later in the book.

7. The couch potato lives on.

Local shops are closing down, and parents often don't let their children out alone because it's not safe. While we are eating more food and more types of food, we are becoming less active. Today there are a lot more things to keep us firmly on the couch, although the term "couch potato" has been around for a long time. Just 20 years ago, TV channels and video games were far more limited than they are today, and humans were still finding reasons to stay seated for as long as possible.

Most children don't even walk to a bus stop but start and finish their school day in the car. Getting very little exercise and playing interactive games on a screen, children are being severely influenced by the *gamification* of modern life. New research suggests that from the age of just seven, children are beginning to enter a "tragic decline" in physical activity long before they leave primary school.

It's recommended that children should be involved in some kind of physical activity for a total of 60 minutes a day, but many children can go through a full day without using up any energy at all.

It's recommended that children should be involved in some kind of physical activity for a total of 60 minutes a day, but many children can go through a full day without using up any energy at all.

8. Nobody is responsible for being overweight or obese.

There's no single reason why obesity rates are so high, but a number of factors around food and lifestyle have combined to cause our current situation. We generally travel by car and have houses packed full of gadgets and devices, which means we don't have to use much energy. At home we sit in front of screens watching a wide choice of TV channels or using a home computer.

The society we now live in has been described as an *obesogenic environment*, which actually increases the risk of becoming obese. Being overweight is not something that children should be made to feel guilty about, and it's important that we keep this in mind as we deal with this problem. Modern society operates in a way that makes staying fit and healthy a challenge, especially for those from lower income backgrounds.

With more people sitting in front of computers all day and fewer doing heavy manual work, our lives have changed dramatically over the space of a generation. The armchair variety of sport is currently winning over the act of actually going out and playing. We have more money to spend on more types of food, but we tend to stick to a select few calorie-rich dishes rather than branching out into more inventive, healthier cooking.

The size and conditions of the people around us, especially the children, should not be blamed on the individual in this kind of atmosphere.

9. Obesity is everybody's problem.

Obesity currently costs the NHS around £1 billion to treat each year, with an overall cost to the economy of up to £2.6 billion. Obese children are likely to be absent from school and underachieve. Society in general – our peers, health service, schools and family – will all be affected by the obesity of individuals in their lives. This is not something that only a select few of us need to worry about.

The NHS, according to some, could eventually be bankrupted by the future cost of treating the obesity epidemic. Colleagues, down the line, will also be impacted when our obese children grow into obese adults with complications which require them to take time off work.

10. Children especially are in danger of becoming obese.

Most parents know about the importance of a balanced diet but it's your responsibility to safeguard your own child from future problems. In the first few years of life, a child's body lays down cells to store fat. If a large amount of fat is stored at this time, a larger number of cells will be created to store the excess fat. Experts believe that obese children may have up to three times as many fat cells as children of a healthy weight, and that once these fat cells are created they will stay with the child for their entire life.

The number of cells that have been created can determine the amount of fat the body tries to store. This means that if you were obese or overweight as a child, your body is programmed to carry a higher amount of fat. While it's possible to lose this weight through diet and exercise, it'll be a very difficult process and would be much easier to simply avoid having this problem in the first place.

With no control over the kind of food they are given, children are very vulnerable when it comes to eating – especially younger children. This is likely to stay with them throughout their lives if patterns of unhealthy eating are established in their childhood. Prevention is much better than the cure for young children. Only you can stop your child from developing weight-related complications later in life.

What have we learned?

- It's everyone's responsibility to deal with the obesity epidemic, but it's nobody's fault that things are the way they are.
- Combining small amounts of exercise with large amounts of food is a bad idea.
- Obesity is a major issue, but there's plenty of support available if you know where to look.
- Obesity has grown out of our changing lifestyle.
- Obesity is a serious medical condition – but can be tackled.

2

What Happens Now?

Survey of Attitudes About Obese Children

We discovered how deep the negative images of overweight children really are in 1961, when an American study entitled "Cultural Uniformity in Reaction to Physical Disabilities" explored the stigmatisation of obese children. It is tempting to think that attitudes have changed since 1961, but when another team did a follow up in 2001, with the obesity rate doubled, they found that children's attitudes had not changed for the better and the same prejudices were still firmly in place.

During the study, pictures of children with various kinds of disabilities were shown to primary school children, who were then asked to rank who they would most and least like to be friends with. The obese child was the person that every child tested said they would least like to be friends with.

The Causes and Effects of Obesity

Children's weight may go up and down for many reasons, for example if they are taking certain types of steroids. Lack of exercise and overeating aren't always the causes of weight gain and obesity in children. Obesity can also be caused by any one of a number of rare conditions. For example, the genetic condition Prader-Willi syndrome can cause a child to develop an excessive appetite and overeat as a result.

Another condition, hypothyroidism (underactive thyroid gland) stops the body from producing the right amount of hormones for the body to function properly. As a result, the individual will develop a slow metabolism, causing them to gain weight.

The Good News About Obesity

There's no reason why children of obese parents should follow suit if they are able to act early enough to deal with the condition. There is some good news about obesity, even though much of this book will sound like doom and gloom. Virtually all the complications caused by obesity in young children and adolescents can be undone by taking simple actions.

A lifetime of health complaints and devastating diseases can be avoidable for many children. Measles and mumps and diseases like that don't work the same way as obesity: obesity is not a thing your child can catch. Before it reaches a point where it can't be ignored, an obese child's weight is likely to have been building up for a long time – months or maybe even years.

A child below the age of 10 will stand a much better chance of losing weight quickly than an adolescent who may grow into an obese adulthood if action isn't taken. Obesity will be much easier to beat the younger you start to tackle it. Acting sooner rather than later will make sure you can slow or prevent any major conditions associated with obesity – though it should be noted that prevention is still much better than the cure.

There's lots you can do as your child grows to help them become a healthy weight.

When Does Obesity Start?

Obesity expert and campaigner Tam Fry underlines the importance of antenatal screening for obese women in pregnancy:

Maternity services really need to pick up women who are dangerously overweight and offer them counselling and advice on what to do.

It's vital for pregnant women to eat well and avoid junk foods: although obesity can kick in at any age, it often starts in the womb. Emphasis should be on quality, not quantity. Eating for two doesn't mean eating for two adults!

Breast milk is gourmet food for babies, containing everything they need to thrive and grow. For six months after a baby is born, doctors recommend that they're given nothing but breast milk. A large amount of research has suggested that breastfeeding lowers the risk of your baby growing into an obese child, while protecting them from any number of different early diseases and conditions.

Few parents would willingly neglect their children and leave them at risk, but children who grow up with unhealthy eating habits and inactive lifestyles are at risk from obesity, which can be so bad as to be life threatening. Doctors have known for a long time that obese children are at risk of developing a number of conditions later in life, including heart disease, some cancers and osteoarthritis. As the stage where a child begins meeting solids and varieties of food, weaning is another important part of your child's development. During infancy it's important to use the information, support and advice available from your health visitor or clinic on weaning and child nutrition. You will give your child the habits of a lifetime at this stage, so it's really important that you set good eating patterns to get them off to a healthy start.

We go to a lot of effort and expense to keep our children safe from danger and give them everything we can, because we want what's best for them. It's worth examining some of the immediate and longer-term health risks associated with obesity in detail, because the issue isn't that parents are actively trying to harm their children. The issue is that many family members, guardians and parents just don't know about the risks that obesity poses.

As a graphic indication of how serious the problem is, recent statistics taken as the rates of obesity in the UK have soared show that a number of diseases which were once considered to be conditions associated with old age have started to occur in children as young as seven.

It's vital for pregnant women to eat well and avoid junk foods: although obesity can kick in at any age, it often starts in the womb.

There is some hope to be found, however, in the form of a recent study conducted in Atlanta by Solveig Cunningham and her colleagues at Emory University. The results of this study have suggested that if a child is able to avoid obesity by the age of five, they have a much stronger likelihood of avoiding obesity and its health complications for the rest of their life.

The Role of Genetics

Obesity is one family heirloom that no one should have to inherit. Although obesity does seem to run through families, this could be because parents are passing on their own unhealthy habits to their children. Obesity may be linked to hereditary conditions in some cases, but that's usually not the only cause. Help your children to avoid the same pitfalls by identifying whether or not obesity is an issue in your family and taking action against the cycle continuing.

What's the Big Deal?

For obese adolescents and young adults there is increased risk of doing badly in school, earning less and being excluded from friendship groups. The effects of obesity can last a lifetime. More than 70% of obese children and more than 85% of obese adolescents will become obese adults, a risk that a child couldn't possibly understand but a parent should take note of.

In adult life, ill health and premature death are much more likely in those who were obese as children.

Long Term – Heart Disease and Stroke

Approximately two thirds of children at primary school age who are obese will have at least one cardiovascular risk factor, and approximately one quarter will have two or more. The processes that lead to cardiovascular disease in later life are strongly associated with child obesity. In the long term, overweight children are at risk of heart disease and stroke as they may be prone to high blood pressure.

These problems will be made worse by an unhealthy diet which is likely to contain high levels of cholesterol. High blood pressure, raised blood fats (lipids) and insulin levels in obese children are all major risk factors for cardiovascular problems.

If obesity is not brought under control, cardiologists fear that the recent successes in reducing the number of deaths from heart disease will be undone. Dr Kristen Nadeau of the CU Cancer Center in Colorado explains:

… The earlier you are exposed to obesity, the earlier we may see the onset of complications including type II diabetes, cardiovascular disease, metabolic syndrome and cancer. That makes sense: these complications don't happen overnight, and the earlier you start the ball rolling, the earlier and more likely you are to see early morbidity and mortality from them.

Short Term Concerns

It's easy to forget that being overweight isn't just about appearing to be fat; it's about being unhealthy and unfit. Obesity in children is not just a cosmetic problem.

Children on a poor diet are likely to be severely constipated. Your child may be pale, spotty, have dry skin patches, suffer chafing or develop fungal infections under folds of skin. If your child is missing out on key vitamins and nutrients, they'll not only look fat but unhealthy in other ways too. Their teeth will suffer and may rot if they consume too many fizzy drinks and sugary snacks. Bad breath and greasy hair may also become issues prematurely, and these can be difficult for a child to manage.

Tiredness, asthma, heat intolerance, shortness of breath on exertion and bone and joint problems are just some of the problems an obese child might experience, as well as the general physical discomfort that comes from being overweight. Type 2 diabetes, high blood pressure and abnormal blood fat levels may also develop. Problems with concentration and learning performance may also occur if your child is one of the large proportion of obese children who suffer from episodes of disturbed breathing during sleep, also known as obstructive sleep apnoea.

Asthma

One of the most important things for children with asthma is keeping fit and healthy, which they are encouraged to do. A child who already has asthma may find that their condition gets worse as their weight increases, as child obesity is associated with an increased risk of asthma. It is very difficult for obese children with asthma to stay healthy.

While obesity can contribute to the development of respiratory conditions like asthma, it's now been found that asthma may also contribute to a child's likelihood of becoming obese. One study found that non-obese children who had asthma were 51% more likely to become obese than non-obese children who didn't have asthma.

Type 2 Diabetes

For more information see *Diabetes – The Essential Guide*.

Children as young as seven have recently been diagnosed with this disease. These children are all clinically obese and face potential blindness, heart disease and amputations. If the insulin produced by your child's body doesn't work properly or is not produced in large enough amounts, they may develop Type 2 diabetes. Being overweight is linked to this condition in the majority of cases. In the UK, according to Diabetes UK, there are estimated to be around 1000 children with Type 2 diabetes, though this type of diabetes has been observed in the USA for some time. The condition was originally associated with middle age.

It is possible to prevent the disease later in life if you get into good eating and activity habits early on to avoid excess weight gain. This type of diabetes is of particular concern for people of South Asian origin.

Treating Type 2 Diabetes in Children

The child and their family will generally be provided with dietary information, and in some cases the child will also be given some pills and a blood test machine to help monitor their blood sugar. Because this condition is tied to a lack of exercise and an unhealthy diet, children with Type 2 diabetes are often treated by being encouraged to take up exercise and eat a more restricted diet.

If the extra weight can be lost early enough, there's a small chance that Type 2 diabetes can be stopped in its tracks. What's more likely, however, is that diabetes will play a major role in their lives right into adulthood.

Cancer

Cancer Research UK suggests that in the UK, 12 thousand people could avoid getting cancer by not being overweight. Cancer of the oesophagus (food pipe), womb, colon, gallbladder and kidney are all more common in those who are overweight. According to Cancer Research UK:

If the extra weight can be lost early enough, there's a small chance that Type 2 diabetes can be stopped in its tracks.

Being obese as a child might directly affect a person's risk of developing cancer as an adult, regardless of what they grow up to weigh. In other words, obesity in early years might be leading to biological changes that make cancer more likely later on.

OSA – Obstructive Sleep Apnoea

Sleep apnoea is a sleep disorder characterised by a lack of oxygen in the blood during sleep. Sleep apnoea is closely linked to being overweight. The condition may make your child a heavy snorer, and will cause them to wake suddenly during the night.

Fatty tissues in the upper airway can cause the tonsils of obese children to become enlarged. During sleep, the upper airway may also be collapsed by fat deposits in the chest and neck. Although sleep apnoea does occur in children of healthy weights, when it occurs in overweight and obese children it's often more difficult to cure.

Psychological Effects of Being Overweight

Children like to join in and belong, but an obese child may be excluded from many of the physical activities that children take for granted. For obese adolescents, particularly girls, the consequences of being obese are worse and can lead to poor self-image. One of the most difficult aspects of obesity to understand and treat is the psychological effect which this exclusion may have, which is far more difficult to resolve than many of the other illnesses obesity may cause.

Being excluded will only make matters worse for obese children, as it will reduce the amount of exercise they might get. Younger children will find themselves in a vicious circle – they may want to join in with sport and games but won't be able to and won't get any benefit from activity and exercise. Sadly, though, many playground games are simply not doable for overweight kids.

A child's developing sense of self and self-esteem may well be negatively impacted by society's view of obesity. Even at very early ages, children will be painfully aware of the negative view their society has towards them.

Going into the teenage years is dangerous for obese adolescents on two scores. Even schools struggle to provide obese youths with opportunities to keep active, especially for teenage girls who are much less likely than boys to get involved (or be invited to get involved) in physical activities.

Once again for these young people, a vicious cycle of lack of exercise leading to obesity leading to lack of exercise will begin. Statistically they are also less likely to be able to combat their condition. A whole different set of negative body images exists for obese young people to contend with, and secondary school can be a dangerous place for negative body image even for those of a healthy weight.

Eating disorders like bulimia, anorexia and binge eating, as well as lowered self esteem and anxiety, are just some of the psychological consequences associated with being overweight. It's not too difficult to figure out why this is the case. Slim, muscular, youthful bodies are worshiped non-stop by modern culture. "Attractive" is a word reserved only for proportional, skinny bodies.

When an obese kid's culture makes it clear that the way they appear is wholly undesirable, it's easy for them to feel bad about themselves, to become anxious or upset or develop eating disorders.

OA – Osteoarthritis

Obese children may find their knees and hip joints ache under the pressure of carrying around so much excess weight. An overweight child's joints may suffer wear and tear beyond their years as a result of the tremendous strain put on them by their weight. The damage will be reversed if the extra weight is taken off the child's joints in time. However, it'll become more difficult for a child to return to full health the longer they stay at an unhealthy weight.

One recent study has suggested that high BMI can increase an individual's risk of developing hip osteoarthritis, knee osteoarthritis and generalised osteoarthritis by 0.4%, 1.3% and 2.7% respectively.

Limited Opportunities

Obese children will be at increased risk of discrimination as a result of their condition, according to one British Medical Association report into obese children's life chances.

What Have We Learned?

- Obesity can be a life-threatening condition, and must be taken seriously.
- We're currently experiencing the highest level of children experiencing early complications as a result of their weight.
- Most of the complications caused by obesity can be halted or reversed.
- It can be the cause of long-term health problems.

3

Facing the Facts

What Is a Healthy Weight?

A healthy weight is one which is appropriate for your child's age and is part of a healthy lifestyle. If you're still not sure about this, speak to your family doctor or practice nurse who will reassure you. It can be incredibly difficult to try and work out a child's healthy weight. Once you finally work out the answer, it'll only remain valid for a few months (or even weeks), as your child will very quickly grow out of their previous measurements.

Children of healthy weights will generally feel and look well, will be able to run and play without their size holding them back, and will have a healthy appetite. Focus on this, and you should be alright. Try to pay no heed to friends, coworkers, neighbours or relatives (unless they're telling you to listen to your doctor!), as they really have no better idea than you do.

Are You in Denial?

Sometimes it's just easier to stay the way you are and not to rock the boat. It's easy for adults to notice changes to their own body size and shape but it's much more difficult to understand what changing shapes mean for children. One major obstacle to tackling a weight problem is parental denial.

This is a big problem for teachers and carers who may be concerned, and an even bigger problem for the child in question. Look through old photos and see how your child's face shape changes over a matter of months and you will see how much variation there can be. Is your child's new puppy fat a temporary change as they gear up for a growth spurt, or are their chubby cheeks a result of their diet?

Parents know that they will be forced to examine their own lifestyles if they admit their child has unhealthy habits, and may go into denial as a result.

Is My Child Overweight or Obese?

When a research team from University College London asked parents in outer London to describe their child's weight, they found some very confused views about obesity. In parents of overweight and obese children in the early years of primary, just 6% correctly identified their child's weight. This was also an issue in parents of older children. Underweight, overweight or obese?

Eating habits, mealtimes, portion sizes and the type of food we eat have all changed so much that it's impossible to say anymore what makes up three square meals a day. The same study suggests that parents' views of acceptable eating habits are based on what their friends and neighbours do, so if they see other families tucking into fast food and ready meals washed down with gallons of fizzy drinks, they think it's acceptable.

Many parents have difficulty telling where their child falls on the weight spectrum. It's really difficult for a parent to form an accurate view of their child's weight. Today's kids are taller and larger than those of previous generations, and an individual child's body shape will change constantly. Parents simply have no idea of what a healthy child looks like, concluded the London research team.

The majority of parents with overweight children just aren't aware of the severity of their child's condition.

The biggest challenge for some families may be to accept that they will only be able to help their child if they try to change some family habits. Negative reflections of the family and their lifestyle is a major concern for some parents, who are reluctant to have their child labelled as "obese" for this reason.

For some families, the solution is simple: they need to listen to their child's concerns about their own weight. Overweight children need to feel supported and in control of their weight, as in many cases they are already aware that they have a weight problem.

Ethnic Risk Groups

See links to resources for ethnic groups on page 109. Unwanted weight gain must be paid particular attention in children from certain ethnic groups. According to *Couch Kids – The Continuing Epidemic*, a report by the British Heart Foundation, boys from the Indian and Pakistani community are at risk of being overweight, while girls from the Pakistani and Afro Caribbean community are more at risk of developing obesity. The chance to exercise is presented less to children from any South Asian community, and these children are four times as likely to be obese than children from the white population.

Why Are Some Schools Weighing and Measuring Children?

This is for government statistics on children's health. Children in the reception and final years of primary schools in England have been having their weight and height measured in school on a voluntary basis since 2007 as part of the National Child Measurement Programme (NCMP). It's up to you whether to get involved in this programme but it might be helpful to tap into the resources the school should be able to offer you. In some cases, warning letters have been sent to parents if their child has been found to be excessively overweight, though any parent can access their child's results if they request them.

Weighing up Your Options

Whether it's by yourself or with the help of your healthcare team, there are many ways you can check and track your child's weight. Below are some of the main options for monitoring weight, though it should be noted that there is a lot of debate over which is the best method.

Whether it's by yourself or with the help of your healthcare team, there are many ways you can check and track your child's weight.

Waist to Height Ratio

The website **www.weightlossresources.co.uk** recommends a way of monitoring a child's size as they grow without using scales, as a means of moving away from the focus on weight.

This method involves measuring your child's waist circumference and height, then dividing the first measurement by the second. For example, if your child is 125cm tall and has a waist circumference of 60cm, the calculation would be 60/125=0.48.

Children who have a waist to height ratio of more than 0.5 are likely to be overweight – and the larger the number, the greater the potential problem. If the waist measurement is half the height measurement – i.e. if the result is 0.5 or higher – this could indicate a potential weight issue.

The best part of this method is that it means you don't need to make a fuss about your child's weight to keep them healthy. It's easy to measure waist circumferences to check sizes for buying new clothes, and most kids love to measure their height to see how much they're growing.

BMI – Body Mass Index

Back in Chapter One, we took a brief look at Body Mass Index. It is calculated by dividing weight in kilograms by height in meters squared. This is a method used to figure out if a person's health is being put at risk by their weight.

BMI is not a failsafe way of calculating whether your child is overweight and results should be interpreted by a healthcare professional. Special-age and gender-specific charts are available (like the ones opposite). These are called centile charts and are plotted to give cut off points, which give a definition of obesity. While a child's BMI is calculated using the same method as that of an adult, adult figures should not be used for children as they don't take into account age and growth patterns.

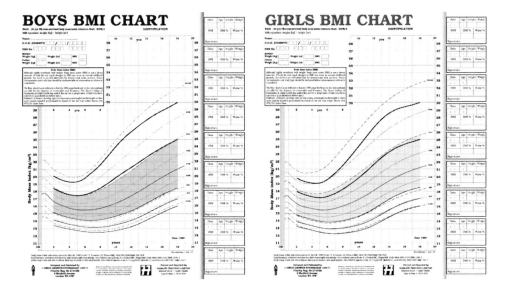

© Child Growth Foundation

Using the UK 1990 reference chart for age and sex, doctors define obese children as those whose BMI is over the 98th centile. Those with a BMI above the 91st centile as defined as being overweight.

The charity Weight Concern has a calculator for children you can use. You can calculate your child's BMI online, just like you can most things by now. The rate at which children grow and change is reflected by the fact that the calculator factors in your child's date of birth and the current date.

From the age of two onwards, it's likely that your doctor will determine your child's BMI at routine checkups, comparing it against those of other kids the same age by plotting it on a chart.

Speaking to Your Child

Some children are interested in their weight but it's important not to make a big issue of this before you start. It's important to consider your child's feelings before you start sizing them up, and we'll talk about how to have this conversation later in the book.

Talking to Your Doctor

It's important not to set too much store by the results of your DIY measuring, tracking and weighing without consulting a health professional, though these methods are still helpful if you want to keep track for your own records. Try to make a point of talking to your pharmacist, your doctor, a practice nurse or health visitor. Professionals will be able to talk you through options that are available to you, offer advice and give you the support you need. Once you've had this discussion, you'll know what changes to make and what results to expect, so your own measurements will be more useful.

Risks for Kids

Professionals will be able to talk you through options that are available to you, offer advice and give you the support you need.

There are certain behaviour patterns that could make your child prone to obesity in the future, even if they don't currently hit the overweight or obese cut off points. These include…

- Being glued to a gaming screen, computer or television for more than two hours a day;
- Getting puffed out easily, and not having an interest in physical activities;
- Consuming large amounts of fatty snacks, crisps, sweets, chocolate and biscuits;
- Having obese siblings and parents;
- Not getting their five-a-day;
- Eating in front of the TV;
- Picking their own food;
- Spending less than 30 minutes a day being active;
- Bingeing on certain foods and having excessive faddy eating habits;
- Not fitting into clothes for their age, especially round the waist.

Becoming Obese

Excess weight will not vanish overnight and it will take time to make changes which achieve results, so it's important for you to start with a positive attitude to help carry your child through. Obesity is an issue that builds up for months or even years, a result of a long-term lifestyle of inactivity and unhealthy eating. Parents of obese children don't just wake up and discover their child has gained an amazing amount of weight overnight.

This Is Nobody's "Fault"

Although we can all certainly do better to help our children, there's no point in blaming Grandma for giving your child too many sweets. Your child's health is something you must not blame on your child or anyone else. However, with the right understanding and attitude you can help them change life for the better. If your child can't eat lunch because the school doesn't have a proper dining room and the children are eating at their desks, it's not their fault. A teenager who eats chips at a college canteen where they only serve chips has little choice.

If a toddler is offered chips and pizza at a birthday party, they aren't going to know how to request a healthier option or even that chips are particularly unhealthy. A kid can't be held responsible for not getting enough exercise if their school only plays team games for which they never get chosen. The "obesogenic environment" is the real cause of your child's condition – the less-than-ideal situation that has made your child the way they are.

What Have We Learned?

- Make sure you're getting your facts about your child's weight from an expert.
- Although it's only one part of keeping your child healthy, keeping track of their weight is a good idea.
- Make sure you aren't in denial about your child's weight. This won't help anyone in the long run.
- There is no such thing as an ideal weight for children, only a healthy lifestyle.
- If your child is not obese, make sure they don't get that way.

Preparing to Deal with Weight Issues

Now it's time to take action! You may have tried to change your child's eating habits in the past or thought vaguely that they could be overweight. You should have a better understanding of why it's important to get your child on track for a healthy lifestyle now that we've discussed some of the facts and the background to obesity. There always seems to be a good reason to put off making changes until tomorrow, even if both you and your child want to make a start. Today we're going to start actually making those changes for the better.

Talking to Your Child

The following advice should be helpful for everyone. If you're making the decision to do something for your child, then you need to think carefully about how you're going to talk to them about it. Bear in mind, and stress to your child if they are old enough, that the situation of being overweight isn't anybody's fault but it's not doing anybody any good and it won't go away without your whole family making some changes. If your son or daughter is already keen to make changes, so much the better!

Every parent wants to give their child the best life possible. Teachers and other individuals involved in childcare will also want what's best for the children in their care, and this can sometimes involve working with parents to have this discussion. Give plenty of thought to what you expect your child to do about the situation, and how you're going to put such a delicate question in words.

It's Vital to Talk

Your child might try risky dieting at some point in their life if their weight issues aren't dealt with in time, and this can be a lot more dangerous than doing nothing. However difficult it is to start the conversation, the problem will not go away if you don't deal with it head on.

Older Children

What they eat is suddenly more in their control when children are between the ages of 7 and 11. From 12 onwards, adolescents will have more understanding about food, weight and body shape, although their knowledge might not be from the best available sources. You'll still need to do a lot of the thinking and decision making for them, but you'll also need their understanding and participation if you want to make changes to their diet.

Decisions about healthy eating and activity should have a lot of input from your older child, who should be able to come up with ideas to help themself.

Little Kids

Action is probably more important than words for younger kids, though every child needs to hear messages about activity and healthy diets. Follow advice from your health visitor and teach them the basics of five a day, a balanced diet and healthy snacking. What they eat is more or less in your control when your child is under the age of five, so this is probably the easiest time to get them eating healthily. Every day, try to make sure your child takes part in some form of physical exercise.

Bringing It Up

If you need to start a conversation with your child about their weight, you could bring up the subject by asking how they feel when…

- Their size is commented on by other people;
- People tease them about their weight;
- They are not able to get involved in sports and games;
- Buying clothes that are for older age groups.

If you know someone who has been in a similar situation, point this out and use them as a good example. Let your child talk and see how far it takes you if your child brings up the subject of weight themself. You can progress to the stage of making plans if the conversation gets there on its own.

It might be helpful to ask your child if they'd like you to help them do something about it, or if it's something that upsets them.

A Word About Energy Density

Most processed or prepared foods are very "energy dense" as they contain added sugar and fats to make them more appealing and last longer. A couple of pieces of chocolate can easily contain as much "energy" or calories as a bag full of lettuce leaves. These days, the amount of energy that gets packed into foods can be pretty difficult to wrap your head around. As many as four thousand calories might be hidden in a takeaway curry meal, while a can of fizzy drink can contain as much energy as a small meal. If you eat simple, homemade food, you can often eat larger meals and still consume fewer calories.

Most processed or prepared foods are very "energy dense" as they contain added sugar and fats to make them more appealing and last longer.

A Question of Mathematics

The energy imbalance is the main reason for unwanted weight gain, and it's a pretty simple concept to understand. You will put on weight if you take in more energy than you use. That's it. What's equally simple is the solution: Burn off more energy, and take less in. This means using up more energy in physical activities, and not necessarily eating less but just eating less of certain food types.

Surgical and Medical Options

There are some options available for the most severe forms of obesity which aren't necessary for those who are simply overweight or mildly obese. These are not methods to take lightly and are a last resort, which will require expert medical advice and support every step of the way. Drugs, stomach stapling and gastric bands are all potential solutions.

With unknown consequences, the idea of using adult drugs and operations to treat childhood obesity is controversial and potentially dangerous. A consultation with your GP is necessary before you even consider looking into these options.

Maintenance or Loss?

Growing children generally have a high metabolic rate compared to adults, and active children have an even higher metabolic rate. Your child may not actually need to lose weight to be healthy – an important distinction between child and adult weight issues. Most children should be able to continue to grow healthily and avoid unnecessary weight gain if they aim to stop gaining weight and start maintaining their current weight through exercise and healthy eating.

What to Avoid and What to Emphasise

The charity Weight Concern have shared the following pieces of invaluable advice. Consider the following when you talk to their child about their weight.

The Word 'Diet'

- Do ask your child how you can help them eat more healthily.
- Don't make your child feel guilty about their eating habits.

A diet is a temporary eating plan which may cause some loss of weight because it generally excludes certain groups of foods. This book, as you may well notice, will not discuss the dreaded "D-Word" in any great detail. Obese or overweight children won't really benefit from things like dieting and slimming. Obese children don't need to "slim down" to an "ideal weight", and even if there was an ideal average weight for their size, it probably wouldn't remain that way for very long.

Cutting out food groups from a growing child's daily intake can be harmful, and it's not something they need to do. Stabilising and maintaining a healthy weight through exercise and a balanced diet is the goal here, not arriving at some "perfect" weight.

What Is the Parent's Role, and How Can They Set a Good Example?

- Do set a good example and do everything that you expect your child to do.

- Don't moan about your own weight and how "boring" being on a diet is.

If you sit on the sofa eating donuts and attempt to tell your child about the importance of healthy living, they may see right through you. The important thing is to lead by example, and you may have to re-think your own habits before trying to change your child's. Your attitudes and approaches can have a positive influence on children, because parents and carers are the most important role models in a young person's life.

Your own lifestyle may need to come under scrutiny if you want to help your child. Schemes like *Small Steps Big Difference*, a healthy eating and activity campaign that targets women in Edinburgh, can be found all over the country. It has an upbeat approach and aims to show women of all ages how they can make small lifestyle changes for the better. Many local councils and health bodies have similar initiatives and are well worth checking out. Help is out there if you look for it! From substituting herbs or spices for sugar and salt, to getting off the bus early to walk a little longer, to choosing a humble piece of fruit over a slice of cake, these programmes have plenty of ideas for how you can take a look at your lifestyle and identify the changes you need to make. Your child is likely to pick up on the changes you make and take an interest if you show enough enthusiasm for getting involved.

The following pieces of advice might be useful if you're talking about the issues of being obese or overweight and want to know how you can help your child…

- You don't know why other people are the way they are, so you should never make negative comments about other people's weights.

- Don't give your child the idea that they can only be happy if they reach some imaginary ideal weight. Don't give them the idea that there's an ideal weight at all.

- Tell your child that it can be difficult for some people to control their weight but the main thing is to have healthy habits.

- Point out that no one is perfect and everyone has good points and attractive features.

There Are No Quick Fixes

Everyone has seen television programmes that take overweight, unhealthy people and turn their lives around. Behind the scenes there will have been a small army of people working away to make this possible. There is also the added motivation of not wanting to fail in front of a million viewers! We meet the "star" around 7 p.m. and understand that this is the desperate lady or gentleman being made over this week.

With a new life, haircut and wardrobe, we meet the same person transformed and two stones lighter by the end of the show, just half an hour later. You can work a bit of magic in your child's life with the right support and knowledge, but it's important to understand that there are no quick fixes or miracle cures. It's not as simple as it looks, even if the transformation we're presented with really did happen. Expert fitness trainers, dieticians, life coaches and doctors will all have worked with the star, devising a strict plan which they had to follow for weeks or even months.

You may well live in an area where they run a special programme for children. Find out what's available and access as much support as you can. You won't have the same team of experts to work with as the people on TV do, but there's still plenty of support out there if you know where to look. Healthy habits of behaviour will need to be learned and used to replace the bad habits you've picked up over the years, and it's the responsibility of you and your child to get this done.

There is a genetic link to over-eating but it could also be due to trauma or distress over a family break-up or school problems such as bullying.

The Psychology of the Overeater

There is a genetic link to over-eating but it could also be due to trauma or distress over a family break-up or school problems such as bullying. Coming to terms with eating habits, according to many adults who have lost weight successfully, becomes a lot easier when you become aware of the reasons for your overeating. If there are certain times he or she overeats in response to particular situations.

Children are unlikely to be quite as self-aware as this, but will have learned their eating habits early in life. One common issue is that of people who "eat their emotions". Parents need to think about how their own behaviour could be picked up by their children and how they could modify it to change the way their children think about food. The attitude of friends and parents towards food, as well as family eating patterns, also play a major role in overeating.

Foods will begin to be associated with nice things and positive emotions in the mind of a child who is given cakes, treats and sweets as regular rewards for good behaviour.

Your child's eating habits are likely to fall into specific patterns – try to understand these.

In certain cases, the key to overeating might be your child's attitude and feelings about food, so it's a good idea to talk about these with a healthcare professional.

Healthy Choices Should Become Second Nature

A child can't be held responsible for giving in to the temptation to binge and gorge on unhealthy stuff when there's so much of it around and it's so easily available. The community, child, school, health services and family should all be involved in the prevention of child obesity. The only choices available to a child could be unhealthy unless everyone involved in caring for them supports their goal to become healthy and provides better options for activity and meals. It needs to be easy for your child to make healthy choices.

Motivation and Self-Esteem

In the short term, it will be difficult, but it's important to keep motivation and morale high. The changes an obese child needs to make will bring about a massive, lifelong improvement. As anyone who has abandoned their New Year's resolutions on January 2nd will tell you, changing the habits you've built up over your entire lifetime is not an easy task.

Your child will get a big sense of achievement when they realise what they've done later down the line. It may also help your child to feel better about themselves if you give them small incentives along the way to better health, which will help them to track and celebrate their progress. These incentives might be things that'll help them feel good about themselves, such as a new haircut or some clothes.

Family Matters

All of the immediate family do need to be on board and understand what you're trying to achieve because it won't work if anyone in the family makes fun or won't join in. It's also a good idea to ask grandparents, aunties and uncles to cut back on the treats they give your child or to replace them with toys, magazines or healthy options. Since families tend to reinforce bad eating habits and sedentary lifestyles, it's logical that they can make good habits acceptable.

Children are generally more successful in controlling their weight and more focussed on their goal when they have the support of their family. Everyone in the family should think about keeping their bad habits to themselves for a while, or (even better!) choosing healthier options for themselves. It may be difficult to get siblings to give up their favourite treats and snacks, though! If they don't support you, it might be a good idea to take family members to one side and talk to them about the consequences you may face if eating habits aren't brought under control.

Don't Focus on the Negatives

Above all, let your child know that they are loved and appreciated and that you're working through this process with them. Tell your child when you notice things you like about them, e.g. a nice smile, a funny joke, a kind thought. The difficult early days will be much more manageable if you boost your child's self-esteem to give them better confidence and morale. Beating obesity shouldn't be the only thing your child has to think about. Make sure you find something your child is good at so they can concentrate on that too.

Help your child to see their worth by highlighting their past achievements. Try making a scrapbook of all of the things they've managed, their talents, their awards, their special qualities. Things like school reports, family photographs and certificates can be physical indicators of what makes your child special.

What Have We Learned?

- When it comes to weight loss, there's no easy way out.
- Your child will benefit the most from this experience if you're able to take the time to talk to them.
- It's important that your child feels appreciated and loved.
- A couple of pieces of chocolate can easily contain as much "energy" or calories as a bag full of lettuce leaves.
- Get the family on board.
- Your child is not going on a diet.

5

Help Is Out There

Sources of Help

Some schools have been working hard to bring about changes for a long time, though it's widely believed that the majority of schools aren't doing enough to promote healthy eating to their students. Your local council also has a role to play and should be able to help you find some fun leisure activities. It's also their responsibility to pay attention to residential and school areas and improve their walking and cycle routes.

Low fat food selections and special ranges for children are also becoming available in a number of supermarkets, who are also on the case and ready to provide parents with information about weight control.

You can expect help from a variety of different organisations, each of which can help you in a different way. We'll look at these organisations in greater detail over the course of this chapter.

Time for Change

It may be worth spending some time thinking about your goals and making plans for success if you and your child are ready to start improving your lifestyles. Every child is different and they will want more of some things and less of others, so be flexible and decide what you can achieve. Try to discuss what might not be useful as well as the things you think might work.

Small Steps to Success

A lot of the organisations, which children come into contact with, have long been aware of the obesity time bomb and are doing their utmost to help. No child should be responsible for dealing with their weight alone, because no child is responsible for being obese.

What Can Your School Do?

No more eating under the beady eye of the teacher – most schools are self-service with a varied menu and the rise of the lunch box means children can be more picky about what they eat. School canteens have changed over the past few decades, just like our home eating habits have.

We learned all about the meals that schools in England were serving up to children on a daily basis back in 2005, when Jamie's School Dinners first aired. A known fan of healthy eating, the chef made it clear that he didn't have a very high opinion of the food available, and made equal numbers of friends and enemies in doing so. By now, schools should be more tuned in to helping children with weight problems, as things have moved on and the majority of schools have finally grasped the importance of healthy eating.

There are wide variations in what's on offer in different parts of the country, but by now most schools are at least striving to help their students reach their recommended 60 minutes of daily physical activity.

The following are just some of the questions you should consider asking your child's schools, and ideas they should be thinking about.

- Does your school have kitchens that can cook healthy meals from scratch?
- Is it possible for parents to come in and sample the food on offer?

- How much do you charge for school dinners?
- Does this school run a cooking club or cooking classes?
- Do you run any special offers?
- How do pupils choose what to eat?
- Where will I find your menus?

Playgroups and Daycares

There's no better place to start than playgroup or nursery when you're looking for support. Anywhere like this – places that care for children – should be taking an interest in their wellbeing and development. Here are some key questions to ask if you're selecting a pre-school for your child.

- Will my child have access to healthy snacks?
- Will my child get to take part in physical activities, games and outdoor projects? Will they get to move around?
- Do the children learn about healthy eating, which foods are good and which to avoid?
- Are the children given plain water or fruit juice?

Your Local Health Board

You should be able to access support from your health visitor, family doctor and practice nurse from your local health centre. Information is generally available in different languages and formats. In order for you to get more help, they should then be able to refer you to other services within your local health board area. It may also be worth visiting your local pharmacy, which should be able to provide support and guidance. Those working for your local health board should be able to…

- Give you long-term advice and support;
- Help you keep your child active through a range of ideas;
- Assist you and your child in setting up goals;
- Give advice on various options and offer useful contacts;
- Come up with some healthy eating suggestions for children;
- Tell you about the benefits of healthy living.

You should be able to access support from your health visitor, family doctor and practice nurse from your local health centre.

Different health boards will be tackling obesity in different ways. For example, in 2016 the health board of Greater Glasgow and Clyde drafted a Child Healthy Weight Framework to identify key intervention areas for each life stage. Ideas included…

- Health visitors providing vital, evidence-based physical activity and infant feeding and weaning advice as part of the universal children's programme;

- Early years intervention based in the home for the most complex/at-risk severely obese children;

- Additional tailored support for the wider psychological and medical needs of overweight older children, with structured intensive interventions;

- Structured group-based intensive programmes for the most overweight early years and primary school children and their parents in community settings;

- Weight management intervention for children with higher weight as part of routine assessments and the tailoring of individual plans in early years.

Local Councils

Schools and many other areas which impact on children's lives fall under the authority of your local council. Councils have responsibility for making sure streets and cycle paths are safe and clean for children to use. They maintain cycle paths, parks and leisure facilities, provide public transport and sports centres. Many sport facilities, daycares, activity clubs, after school clubs, playgroups and other services which your child will use are provided and licenced by the council.

Activities and special programmes for overweight children and their families are run by many local councils, so it's worth finding out if there's one in your area. The list is endless: mountaineering, skating, sailing, skiing… there's lots more to do than just running on a treadmill in your local gym!

Healthy living initiatives have also been suggested which would involve councils working with local businesses and stores to encourage healthy choices, and making sure that all cafés that fall under their jurisdiction are serving healthy options.

Those living in England can find out what their local councils are doing to combat the obesity epidemic by reading the LGA publication "Healthy Weight, Healthy Futures" (**https://www.local.gov.uk/healthy-weight-healthy-futures-local-government-action-tackle-childhood-obesity-0**). Similar actions are being taken in Scotland by ScotPHO, in Wales by NHS Wales and in Northern Ireland by ROPIG.

"Some are focussing on getting children physically active and the latest figures suggest less than one in four children are achieving the required levels. Meanwhile, others are concentrating on food and diet. In doing so, they are forging important partnerships with early years settings, schools, community groups and local businesses. But the evidence from councils suggests we should be prepared to be tough too. Liverpool City Council has taken on the food industry, by naming and shaming products that are high in sugar." Local Government Association

Online Resources

Visit parenting sites and join forums where you can exchange experiences and ideas. It's worth spending a bit of time surfing for your own sites, but there are some very useful contact details and online resources listed in the final chapter to help start you off. If you are looking for more specialised advice, for example if you belong to a particular ethnic or faith group or if you have special dietary requirements, then the NHS website should be able to help you out.

Subscribe to feeds to keep yourself updated, and make a separate folder in your bookmarks to keep all of your healthy eating resources in one place. You're sure to be able to pick up some useful tips, and much of it will be anonymous and free to access.

Keeping Track of Your Meals and Activities

Doing nothing for a week or two may well be the best way to start making changes! For the first week, don't introduce any changes but get your child to keep an activity diary. Ask your health visitor or clinic if they have any copies of food and activity diaries they recommend. Take note of things like swimming lessons, playing, walking to school and PE. Write down all forms of exercise, games or activities they take part in, as well as everything they eat. Be honest about it!

Whether you complete the food & activity diary online or on the back of an envelope, once you have completed it, use the information to see where you can make changes. There are loads of diaries like this one (**www.lnds.nhs.uk/Library/Foodactivitydiary. pdf**) online. For older children you may need to fill in the form for them, or find a suitable format online or download an app.

Another great example is available through WebMD. You can download and print it at (**www.webmd.com/diet/printable/food-fitness-journal**). This is a site with loads of great information about diet, exercise and any other health question you could possibly think of. Well worth checking out! Aim for some easily achievable swaps and substitutions in the first week – you might want to swap a couple of fizzy drinks for fresh juice, or a chocolate bar for a bunch of grapes.

If you want to see how much your child changes over the coming weeks, it's a good idea to take videos or photos of them before they start their food diary so you'll have something to look back on. Take note of things you think you might be able to change, and start making a plan. It's also a good idea to include how your child is feeling and any changes they may notice – feeling less tired, feeling fitter, having more energy, clearer skin – as this will show the benefits of the new lifestyle.

You might want to include weight, BMI and waist circumference on the plan at the start to chart your child's progress. Whether it's bouncing on the trampoline or just walking around the block, make sure you include some activity in your child's plan. Make sure that the weight loss element isn't overstressed or given too much importance in the early days.

It's important to make your child aware that you recognise the great progress they're making, as motivation is vital when it comes to getting a child up and running.

Rewarding Your Child's Achievements

When you see your child making healthy choices, let them know how pleased you are. It's important to make your child aware that you recognise the great progress they're making, as motivation is vital when it comes to getting a child up and running. Try rewarding your child with a small present if they get lots of points on the action plan. Try not to use the rewards as bribes, "if you eat that broccoli, I'll give you a new set of pens" – keep the rewards as a surprise instead.

A magazine, some new pyjamas, a small toy or cosmetics are all great rewards. You can break the connection between unhealthy treats (like sweets) and rewards for good behaviour if you give them healthy or non-edible prizes, all the while letting them know how well they are progressing.

What Have We Learned?

- Make the most of the support that is available to you.

- Be realistic about what you can achieve, and plan for the successes you aim for.

- Your child is trying hard at being healthy: make sure you recognise and reward their effort.

- You can expect help from a variety of different organisations, each of which can help you in a different way.

- Make sure all the places where your child spends time are sympathetic to their needs.

- Keep your child's food diary as honestly as possible.

6

Start at the Very Beginning

Leave It on the Shelf

Just leaving these things on the shelf will have a positive impact on your child's weight. They're things that you should try to remove from your child's diet as early as you can.

Sweets and Treats

It's not realistic to expect your child to give up their weekly sweets but try to limit them to small amounts after meals. From bargain bars of chocolate to multi packs of jelly sweets, children's pocket money seems to be stretching further and further and affording more and more unhealthy treats. Don't help your child to associate sweeties with good behaviour – don't hand them out as rewards and prizes. If you keep them out of the house, you'll avoid temptation! It's also a good idea to ask your friends and relatives not to buy them for your child.

Pies, Pastries, Cakes, Biscuits and Sausage Rolls

Children love the flaky pastries of sausage rolls, pies and pastries but you will need to avoid giving these out as snacks between meals. There's no way of telling what's in a cake or a pie, but you can rest assured that they'll be very high in fat and sugar. Savoury pastries can very easily make up part of a main meal, but shouldn't be handed out whenever they tickle your child's fancy. The same goes for cakes and biscuits – these are desserts, not snacks!

Soda! Pop! Carbonated Beverages!

Dietician Laura Stewart suggests that fizzy drinks can often be the main culprit in overweight and obese children.

"Children often consume so much carbonated drink that they are taking in more than their recommended daily calorie intake. These drinks are empty calories and a child who drinks one with lunch will be filling up on a high calorie sugar cocktail and probably won't want to eat any food."

The fizzy drinks industry was worth about £15.7 million in 2015 and continues to grow, according to the British Soft Drinks Association. Children and teenagers tend to get attached to their favourite brand, and are the main consumers of soft drinks.

In this case, less is definitely more. You could give them a low sugar flavoured water or fizzy mineral water. At the end of your child's meal, you can allow your child to have a small glassful of their favourite drink if they're absolutely incapable of cutting it out altogether. Younger children and teenagers should also be avoiding caffeine, which can be found in many of these drinks.

Fats... What Are the Facts?

"Good" and "bad" fats are discussed in the media all the time. But what does that even mean?

Saturated fat is the type that can increase the risk of heart disease because it raises cholesterol. This is the unhealthy or "bad" fat that you find in processed foods and ready meals like burgers, biscuits, cakes and pies. The body needs good fat to carry out healthy maintenance, and finds it in things like nuts, seeds and oily fish.

One type of fat is particularly bad for you, to the point where it's been referred to as "killer fat". It is used to bulk out and preserve sweets, biscuits, takeaways, ready meals and cakes. This is trans fat, a fat which has been converted from vegetable oil to a longer life fat through an industrial process. Trans fats are banned from food use in some countries but not the UK, despite the fact that doctors and health campaigners have been urging the government to ban them for the last decade.

Look out for trans fats and avoid them. "Hydrogenated oil" is another name for this fat which is more commonly mentioned in labelling. It has no nutritional value. However, evidence is stacking up that shows they cause any number of health problems from stroke to infertility to heart disease.

Each year, according to the British Heart Foundation, a child who eats one packet of crisps a day will consume around one litre of oil.

Crisps

Don't make these a daily staple – try not to let children snack on them, offer an alternative for lunch boxes, split a packet between two or three or serve on the side of a meal with a salad. Each year, according to the British Heart Foundation, a child who eats one packet of crisps a day will consume around one litre of oil. These snacks are also packed with sugar (yes, you read that right), salt and additives.

Can't Cook, Won't Cook?

Dietician Laura Stewart, who runs a weight loss clinic for children, suggests that lack of cookery skills could be a big hurdle to eating healthily, and if we are to beat the obesity epidemic we need to know how to do it. Basic cookery need not be time consuming. Many people find that their skills in the kitchen are limited to programming the microwave, however much they enjoy food and cookery shows.

But properly cooking for your family is much healthier, more affordable and more rewarding than takeaways and ready meals.

"Once you learn how to cook quick and easy food, you'll find it's a lot quicker than putting something in the microwave. You can whip up a healthy chicken and couscous a lot quicker than it takes you to heat something in the microwave. "It always amazes me how unaware some people are about the impact certain foods can have on them and their families. It can be as easy as substituting herbs and lemon juice for salt to season your food and a piece of fruit instead of crisps – just a little change can be so beneficial in the long run." Jacqueline O'Donnell

The idea that ready meals, or "dingables", are more convenient than healthy home-cooked meals is a myth, according to Chef Jacqueline O'Donnell. O'Donnell owns The Sisters restaurants in Glasgow, regularly appears as a guest on BBC Radio Scotland's morning show, and runs a healthy eating class for parents.

Get the whole family involved in cooking their meals and have competitions to see who can make the most popular dish in the family. You're not aiming to be a top chef, but once you've mastered the basics you'll be more confident and will have a much more varied menu. Try finding out if there are any evening courses in your area that you could do with an older child, because brushing up on your cookery skills really is worth the effort.

Delia Smith and Jamie Oliver have both written books for people starting from scratch, so a basic cookery book will do if you can't find a suitable course.

The Best Sort of Food Is:

- Organic
- Home-grown
- Cooked properly
- Simple
- Unadulterated

Get your children involved in growing healthy vegetables and fruit if you have a garden. If not, try getting an allotment where the whole family can enjoy the outdoors and get some exercise, or even just grow herbs and salad leaves on your windowsill or hanging baskets.

Learn What You Can about Your Food

Look out for farmers' markets, independent shops, farm shops, or pick your own. There's bound to be somewhere in your area that will allow you to buy fresh produce, and this is a great way of getting back to basics with your food. Lots of local initiatives to increase access to sustainable, healthy and safe foods are promoted through projects like Food Vision, which started in 2000. Food Vision will have something useful for you, as it acts as a hub for all things food related in the UK. Look them up, whether you're looking for mobile fresh food deliveries in Northern Ireland, community gardening in Glasgow or cookery classes in Manchester.

Make a Meal of Meals

Sit down at a table together! You can make it as fancy as you like, but try to get everyone involved in helping, whether it's cooking, setting the table or clearing away. You don't have to whip out the good china every night, but it's a nice idea to do something a little special for at least one meal each week.

The Basics of Healthy Eating

Much has been written about children and their food – enough to fill a whole book on the subject – but if you understand the basics, you can easily start to make the small changes that lead to success. Eating healthily isn't always as simple as we might expect. We know a lot more about exotic dishes and have a much bigger choice than ever before, but we seem to have lost an understanding of the very basics of food and healthy eating.

Every primary school student knows about the "five-a-day" rule, and everyone understands that we should be eating healthily, yet somehow it's still an uphill struggle at times. Older children in particular will have quite sophisticated tastes, but even very young children have a strong idea of what foods they do and don't like.

Before thinking about what to do with it, it's a good idea to learn some very basic facts about the foods we eat.

Back to Basics

If you get the proportions right, you'll be on your way to establishing a very basic but important meal time eating pattern. The following image illustrates the different food groups into which our food is divided, and how much of each group we should be eating.

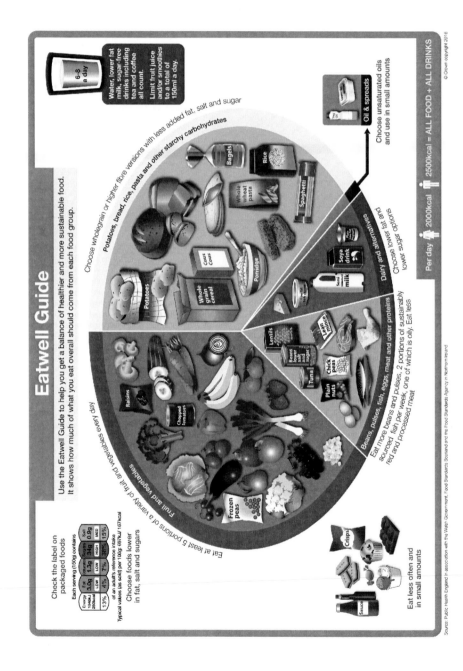

Healthy Eating on a Plate

Each food group is important for children and none should be left out entirely. If you want to give your child the right mix of foods in the right amounts, you'll need to balance your food groups in the right proportions.

Know Your Food Groups

Drink

To save young teeth, restrict juice to mealtimes. To keep themselves hydrated, your child should be drinking up to eight glasses of water every day. As much as possible, fizzy drinks need to be reduced or avoided altogether.

Milk and Dairy

Under twos should have full-fat varieties but older children should use skimmed or semi-skimmed milk. Children and teenagers with growing bones need to be getting plenty of calcium, which you can find in milk and cheese.

Fruit and Vegetables

Controlling weight is much easier if your child's diet is full of fruits and vegetables, which contain lots of important vitamins and fibre. Smoothies and fresh juice count towards your five a day, as well as frozen, tinned, dried and (of course) fresh fruit and veg.

Starches

Starchy food keeps energy levels up through the day. Things like cereal, rice, pasta, potatoes and bread all fall into this category. The spreads and sauces that often go with these foods can be fattening, but the starches themselves are not. Just pay attention to your toppings!

Proteins

This food group includes meat, fish and vegetarian alternatives. Low fat and vegetarian alternatives include legumes, tofu, lentils and eggs. Energy, growth and healing won't happen if a diet doesn't contain enough protein. Once or twice a week, your child can also try oily fish like mackerel or tuna.

Fats and Sweets

Sugar is not forbidden but is so common now that we take much more than we need. Many types of ready meals, snacks and biscuits contain excessive amounts of nasty things like trans fats, which should be avoided. However, a certain amount of fat is needed for a healthy diet. To get their weight under control, you and your child will need to really cut down on these things.

Using This Information

Here are some tips to help you use food groups now that you know what makes them up:

Many types of ready meals, snacks and biscuits contain excessive amounts of nasty things like trans fats, which should be avoided.

- Meals should be based around starchy foods like bread, pasta, rice and potatoes. Always remember that under fives should not be eating brown pasta or brown rice.

- Aim for more than five pieces of fruit and vegetables a day – this is just a minimum recommendation!

- Watch for artificial sugars in yoghurts, and try to choose low fat varieties of milk and other dairy products when you can.

- Later in the book, we'll give you recipes to make your own chicken nuggets and burgers. Kids love these, and they're way healthier than the ones you'll buy!

- Aim for variety! Try not to overload a plate with too much of one food group, and keep an eye on your portion sizes.

- It's easier to keep track of your family's eating habits if you all sit down together for family meals.

- Cut back on ketchup and sauces – you may use these to add taste but they are also adding sugar and additives.

- Eat a healthy breakfast every day, cereal is fine but should be low sugar and accompanied by a portion of fruit.

- Try to choose low fat versions of burgers and sausages, and grill or barbecue rather than fry.

- Avoid high sugar and high fat foods, deep fried foods and takeaway pies and pastries which may contain excessive amounts of fat and sugar.

- Make the most of foods with plenty of fibre, such as fruit and vegetables, oats, grains, seeds, beans, peas and lentils.

Shop Smarter

You will need to take a long look at what goes in your trolley if you want to start helping your child. Week in, week out, many of us buy the same things over and over again when we do our weekly shop in the supermarket.

Things like encouraging overconsumption of the wrong type of food, advertising junk food to kids and limiting choices have drawn a lot of criticism towards supermarkets over the last decade. The good news is, there's now a lot of helpful information available if you know what to look for. See what information they have or ask where you can get more. Try asking about reduced sugar and fat-free ranges next time you go shopping. There's plenty of information online and in most supermarkets, and all major supermarkets will have their own healthy eating ranges.

What's a Little, What's a Lot?

A quick way of working out whether a food you're looking at is right for you is to read the basic nutritional information – things like how much fat and sugar it contains. Here's a quick guide to help with healthy choices, as most people won't actually have a good understanding of what all these numbers mean…

- A little fat is 3 grams per 100 grams.
- 20g or more per 100g is a lot of fat.
- A little sugar is 2 grams or less per 100 grams.
- 10g per 100g is a lot of sugar.

This should give you a better idea of what to avoid. Everything that falls between these numbers is moderate.

Get Fluent in Labelese

The Food Standards Agency has devised a "traffic light" system that many supermarkets, although not all, have adopted. Check out which system the supermarket you shop in uses and try to familiarise yourself with the basics. An ingredients list, GDAs (Guideline Daily Amounts) and other basic nutritional information will be displayed on a panel on the packaging of most foods sold in your local shop. All of this information is put there so that you can tell at a glance what's in your food before you decide if you're buying it or not.

Websites like **www.food.gov.uk** have all of the information you need about the traffic light system and other nutritional guidelines.

Don't Fall for Pointless Buzz Words

Watch out for the following phrases. While the law says that food manufacturers have to be truthful in their packaging, these descriptions are worded to be as vague as possible.

- Reduced fat;
- Helps maintain a healthy diet;
- Extra fruit;
- Natural, organic;
- No added sugar.

If something has "reduced fat", it can still be fattening because of the amount of sugar it contains. Phrases like this may sound good, but they don't actually tell you anything useful about the food you're eating.

What Have We Learned?

- It's a good idea to learn how to cook.
- Educate yourself on how to read supermarket labels and how to know which foods to leave behind.
- Don't fall for meaningless buzzwords.
- Cut back on fizzy drinks and crisps.
- Small steps make for big progress.

7

Take Action!

Making Healthy Eating Happen

Although you all may be very keen to start with, you will need to plan your food so that your new habits become routine and a normal part of family life. If you generally rush around the supermarket on auto-pilot, grabbing the same old favourites and stocking up with handy snacks and special offers, whether you want them or not, you might want to spend a bit of time planning for what you buy.

Keeping your child on course will take a little more than good intentions. Getting into better eating and removing all of the junk from your lifestyle will take a number of practical decisions.

Shopping for Success

Give some thought to your lunch box foods, dinners, desserts, snacks and side dishes. Think about getting a few healthy alternative snacks such as crackers, breadsticks, low fat spreads, raisins and other dried fruit and nuts (assuming no nut allergy) that you can start to offer as alternatives to chocolate, biscuits, sweets and crisps. If you make a gradual change to healthy foods, it should be easier to adapt, particularly if your child is offering the suggestions.

Keep substituting the unhealthy stuff with things your child has agreed to try. Be fairly detailed and think about your child's food diary and anything they might have suggested changing to you. It's a great idea to plan your meals for the week ahead before going to the supermarket. Try to stick to the shopping list you write. It doesn't have to be that ambitious at first, just get into the practice of planning.

Think of all the unhealthy foods in your house and aim to swap them for healthier foods until there's none left.

Offer your alternative snacks as often as it takes, and try not to worry too much about your child's reactions. Stay calm and don't make a fuss.

Kids and Counting Calories

The amount of calories a child needs varies enormously throughout different stages of his or her life. Sometimes children consume more and sometimes they may need to consume more if they are particularly active. It's not helpful to get fixed ideas about eating at this stage. So far we've been careful to avoid the idea of kids counting calories because we don't want anyone to think that dieting is the best plan for a child.

Things like growing and living can't happen without their fuel – calories. As a rule of thumb, the average, active 10-year-old shouldn't really be taking more than 2000 calories per day. Not being active enough to burn off any excess calories they consume is where a child may start having difficulties.

In most cases, fast-food takeaways, ready meals, snacks and sweets and treats are to blame. It all adds up and while busy lives might mean we often have to rely on ready meals and fast foods, home cooked dishes are likely to be much lower in fat than anything you would buy outside the home. If a child is getting a lot of extra calories, you need to ask yourself where all this extra energy is coming from. Around 300-400 calories will be found in a half litre of fizzy drink, while a large burger meal in itself can contain more than 2000 calories.

Experts suggest learning to cook is as important as learning to keep clean and brush teeth for a child. If you're able to cook, this is a valuable skill you can pass onto your kids. It's really important that young children have access to healthy, home-cooked meals. You should think about the food you're buying for your child on a regular basis, even if you aren't that interested in cooking yourself.

Stick with It

The habits of a lifetime are hard to break, but make sure your child knows why you are doing this and that you will keep trying. Even if your first efforts only get as far as cutting back a bag of crisps and a fizzy drink every week, this is something you can build on and it's important to keep going. Don't give up, though it may feel like an uphill battle.

My Child's a Fussy Eater

Children won't starve if you explain that the food you have prepared is the only food that's available. It's better if parents don't encourage their children to develop faddy habits by accepting what they say. It's up to you to encourage your child to keep trying new varieties of foods and in different combinations. The fact is, children are not born with food preferences any more than they are born wanting to wear a seat belt.

So why would you allow them to eat food that can harm them if you wouldn't let them go in a car without strapping in? It feels a lot like kids are being allowed to get fussier and fussier about what they'll eat and what they'll refuse. Many children have a list as long as history of all of their likes and dislikes. If your child says something like "I don't like ham", it's most likely they're thinking of a particular time when they've eaten some kind of ham and didn't like the taste.

You're risking creating a vicious cycle if you give in and let your child dodge food that's good for them. Unless there's a genuine food allergy then there's no reason not to experiment – everyone has some foods that they don't love, but that doesn't mean they can't eat them.

Here are some suggestions for dealing with your finicky eaters. It's not easy, it'll be frustrating at the beginning, but it'll be well worth it in the end.

- Some kids are fussy eaters just to get attention – is this the case here? Let your child feel involved in choosing their food by working with them on their food diary.

The habits of a lifetime are hard to break, but make sure your child knows why you are doing this and that you will keep trying.

- This is not a café… or is it? A fun exercise is to try and run your kitchen like a café for a week. Employ your kids to clear away, prepare food, wait on tables and wash up, and set opening times and weekly or daily menus. They might even forget about their fussy eating if they're having enough fun!

- Lucky dip snacks – get your child to pick their snacks out of a bag without looking at it. Include lots of different types of snack, and make sure your child eats whatever they've pulled out.

- Do blind tasting – get your child to try small pieces of fruit, vegetables or cheese and see if they can identify it. They might even get a taste for it!

- Try not to think about all the things your child won't eat. Look at what they will eat and build on it – don't let them reject things without trying them first.

Ideas to Get You on the Road to Health

You might like to try the British Nutrition Foundation which has some great recipes available online and by post. You're going to find food suggestions and healthy recipes all over the place – there's no shortage of them!

To get you going, here are some child-friendly food ideas!

Your Own Ready Meals

Pasta sauces, soups, curries and chillies can all be made in large quantities to make sure you always have something healthy to hand if you ever need to save time on cooking. Portion-sized tupperware will allow you to freeze these in just the right amounts.

Super Quick Ideas

Try these if you're super busy:

Stir Fries

With noodles, lean beef or chicken and a supermarket stir fry mix, this dish can be ready in a few minutes. For vegetarian options, opt for tofu!

Chef salad

For a main meal, slice up cheese and cold meats and mix with salad leaves. Drizzle it all with a low-fat salad dressing.

Topped toast

Simple and super-speedy! Choose from a poached egg, baked beans, low-fat cheese or any healthy option for a quick evening meal. Serve with sliced tomato on wholemeal toast.

Omelette

Try to master making a good omelette and then add any type of vegetable or cooked meat and serve as a main course.

Caesar salad

Use a bag of salad leaves and a hot ready roasted chicken, strip off the white meat and mix with salad. Toast a slice of wholemeal bread for croutons and use low fat dressing.

Breakfast

If your child wants to eat healthily, breakfast is a must-have. So what's on the menu?

Low-sugar breakfast cereal

(Don't forget: Children over two should use semi-skimmed milk!) – Either as a side dish or topping, try to add a small handful of chopped fruit like banana, grapes or apples.

Boiled egg and wholemeal soldiers

Sliced tomatoes or carrot sticks can also be fun to dip.

Smoothie

This will only take a second if you have a blender. Use strawberries, pears or any other soft fruits you have in the kitchen, and top up with fresh fruit juice.

Porridge

You can microwave to save time. Use semi-skimmed milk and honey or low sugar jam to serve. Add some fruit on top or on the side.

Try introducing a glass of **unsweetened juice**.

Speedy Lunches

Need something quick and tasty for school holidays and days off? Try…

Cheese on toast

Get yourself a nice, low-fat cheese and some wholemeal bread. Serve with salad, olives, or some low-fat coleslaw.

Homemade houmous

Serve with strips of wholemeal pitta, carrot, bell pepper and cucumber.

Lentil soup with wholemeal bread.

Large Lunch or Evening Meal

These are ideas you can use for whichever acts as your main meal of the day. Steamed vegetables or salad can be served at the side.

Jacket potato

Speed up the process by cooking in the microwave, and use low-fat coleslaw, beans or cheese as a topping.

Simple pizza

A great recipe for this will be given later on. Your child can create their own pizza, and choose their own healthy toppings.

Macaroni cheese or cauliflower cheese

You can use a sauce mix for the cheese but check the ingredients to ensure there are no hidden nasties.

Homemade chicken nuggets

Use the recipe provided, ditch the chips and serve with rice.

Afters

Eating healthy doesn't mean all puddings are off the menu! Try things like…

Fruit

Share a bunch of juicy grapes between the family, or let your child choose their own favourite fruit.

Low fat chocolate desserts or healthy yoghurts

Supermarkets have lots of great yoghurts and desserts for your fridge. Just make sure they aren't packed with sugar!

Fruit salad

Make your own from apples, strawberries, kiwis, grapes – whatever you have to hand. Use juice to sweeten and serve with low fat ice cream.

Sides

Balance the meal and help your child to get a more varied diet by including two or three small sides with each main dish.

Replace chips with **couscous**, **rice** and **bulgur wheat**.

Green leaves

A full blown salad might be a bit much for your child, but they should be able to handle a few salad or rocket leaves. Dress with lemon and add cherry tomatoes for a bit of sweetness.

Canned corn works if you're in a rush, but **corn on the cob** is a healthy and fun side if you can get it.

Steamed vegetables

Choose whatever vegetables your child will eat and steam lightly so they are crisp and crunchy.

Dry roasted slices of potatoes or boiled new potatoes.

Beverages

If your child won't give up fizzy drinks, allow one small glass but encourage them to try carbonated or a fruit flavoured water. You can fill your child's five-a-day quota by serving a smoothie or fresh juice as a drink with their meal, but water is always the best option.

Just Enough vs. Too Much

Don't overload your child's plate and consider using smaller plates to make meals look bigger. We expect far more on our plates than ever before, so portion sizes have got steadily bigger. Some experts theorise that this is one of the causes of our sharp increase in obesity. If needs be, your child can always ask for seconds.

Go Easy on the Sauce

Check the labels and go for low fat, reduced salt varieties and use sparingly. Additives, salt, sugar and fat can all sneak into your child's food through things like barbecue sauce, salad dressings, gravy, mayo and ketchup. They may make the food look more attractive to your child, but they aren't worth it!

Packed Lunches

The Food Standards Agency estimates that children in the UK eat over 5.5 billion lunch boxes every year – almost three-quarters of these contain crisps and only half contain fruit. Going back to the healthy plate, it's easy to achieve a healthy balance by being careful. If you want to ensure your children are given healthy options at lunchtime, there's nothing better than a packed lunch. These are popular with schools and kids alike.

You miss the chance to give your child a healthy balance when they need it most if you fill their lunchbox with pre-packed foods – however convenient these options may be.

Give These a Miss:

- Sodas and pops;
- Pastries and cakes;
- Crisps and salted roasted nuts;
- Chocolate and sweets.

You can fill your child's five-a-day quota by serving a smoothie or fresh juice as a drink with their meal, but water is always the best option.

What Should I Include?

- At least one portion of fruit or vegetables. This can be a carrot, some salad or a piece of your child's favourite fruit.

- Starches – Try to include something like rice, pasta or bread every day.

- Always give your child a healthy drink, like a smoothie or some still water.

- Milk and dairy – don't buy processed cheese, instead use dough cutters to make your own shapes. Include skimmed milk or a low fat yoghurt.

- Meat or fish – tuna is a good option but you could also use cold meat on a wholemeal roll or hummus as a vegetarian alternative.

Outside the House

If you are out and about looking for lunch, avoid the chip shop and the takeaways – buy bread rolls, cheese and fruit from the supermarket for a picnic. Give your child a healthy snack before setting off so they are not tempted too much and get into the habit of carrying fruit or healthy alternatives for when you're out and about. It's best to get your child's carers on board with what you're trying to do if your child is away from home, whether they're at an after school club, extracurricular activity or relative's house.

It might be easiest for your child to avoid unhealthy foods if you pack them a healthy lunch box, instead of relying on other people to make the right call. All the same, as long as they're eating healthily at home, it's not the end of the world if your child ends up at a birthday party that only serves chips, cakes and biscuits.

If your child gets tempted by fizzy drinks, it's also a good idea to make sure there's a bottle of water to hand for a healthier option.

Snacks for Beginners

On average around 1.3 million youngsters spend £1.52 every day on chocolate, crisps and fizzy drinks – before reaching the classroom. Buying snacks on their way to school leads children in Great Britain to spend £413 million every year, according to research carried out by breakfast cereal maker Kellogg's.

You really need to limit your child's intake, because children love unhealthy things like sweets, fizzy drinks and crisps. Look for healthier varieties and replace crisps or chocolate with fruit. Your child won't be so easily tempted if you don't stock up on treats and unhealthy snacks.

Here are some ideas that might help your child's snack addiction. Snacks have become a massive part of being a child so this won't be easy, but it's very possible and very worth it.

- For after school snacking, invest in some small tupperware pots that you can fill with raisins, nuts (if appropriate), apricots and other dried fruits.
- Look out for healthier alternatives to crisps like rice cakes, *Ryvita*, crackers with low fat cheese, oatcakes or crisp breads.
- Whizz up a filling, healthy smoothie using semi skimmed milk, bananas and other soft fruit.
- Try to get out of the habit of giving children treats and snacks as rewards if you want to stop them from associating them with good behaviour.
- Wholemeal toast spread thinly with low fat spread is a quick and filling snack.
- Low fat popcorn is a good idea – children will love seeing it made if you buy some unpopped.
- Switch to low fat, salt and sugar products and try to buy in smaller quantities. It's not the end of the world if you run out.

Simple Recipes

These recipes are so simple even a child can use them (under supervision)! They've all been tried and tested, and are perfect for people whose cooking skills are a little rusty.

Fruit Salad

Cut up grapes, strawberries, bananas, apples and any other fruit you can find in your kitchen. Mix all of the chopped fruit together in a bowl. Add in a glass of orange juice for sweetness, and a dash of lemon juice to keep the fruit from browning. Serve with low-fat ice-cream.

Simple Sushi

You will need...

6 tortilla wraps (white or wholemeal);
Soft french cheese, cream cheese or houmous to spread on the wraps;
Small pack of smoked salmon or fish paste.

Method

Spread cheese or houmous onto a wrap, then apply a thin layer of fish paste or smoked salmon. Roll the whole thing up into a cigar shape, and slice into sections that resemble pieces of sushi.

Easy Pizza (serves five)

You will need...
Dough:

8 ounces of self raising flour;
1 tablespoon of sunflower oil;
6 tablespoons of milk.

Tomato sauce:

Creamed tomatoes or tomato puree;
Salt and pepper;
Low fat mozzarella;
Garlic.

Method

In a bowl, mix together the milk, oil and flour. Turn the mixture onto a wooden board and knead. Cover it with cling film or a clean tea towel, and leave it to rest for 10 minutes. Roll the dough out onto a 10-inch pizza plate or two 7-inch cake tins. Prepare the tomato sauce by combining the tomatoes, garlic and seasoning. Spread this on the pizza bases and add mozzarella. Cook it all together in a medium oven for 15-20 minutes.

Homemade Tomato Soup

You will need...
1 medium carrot;
1 stick of celery;
1 pint of vegetable stock;
Plenty of salt and pepper;
Sunflower oil for frying;
1 tablespoon crème fraiche (optional);
1 can plum peeled tomatoes;
1 onion.

Method
This recipe is really easy, so it's perfect to make with your kids. Chop the carrot, onion and celery finely, and fry them together for five minutes. When the vegetables are softened (but not brown!), add in your salt and pepper, tomatoes and stock. Stir it all together, and leave it to simmer for 25 minutes. Allow the soup to cool a little before blending with a hand blender.

For cream of tomato, add the crème fraiche.

Low Fat Coleslaw (serves five)

You will need...
1 medium red onion;
¼ red or white cabbage;
Low-fat mayonnaise;
Lemon juice;
1 large carrot.

Method
Into a bowl, finely chop the cabbage and the onion. Grate the carrot and add a tablespoon of lemon juice and two tablespoons of mayonnaise. Season to taste.

This can be used with a baked potato, in sandwiches, as a side dish or with salads.

Smoothie

For one large smoothie or two small smoothies, use one banana, three or four smoothies, any other soft fruit of your choice and combine with half a pint of semi-skimmed milk. Do not sweeten. Blend them all together for 30 seconds.

Healthy Red Lentil Soup (serves five)

You will need...

1 medium brown onion;
1 low-salt vegetable or chicken stock cube (dissolved in 1 pint of water);
1 tablespoon of rapeseed or sunflower oil;
Salt & pepper to taste;
2 tablespoons of tomato puree;
1 mug of red lentils.

Method

Finely chop the onion and fry in oil until soft. Dissolve the puree in a mug of hot water and add to the pan. Rinse the red lentils in a sieve. Add these to the pan along with the stock and seasoning. Bring it all to the boil, then simmer for 30 minutes or until the lentils have all broken down. If you want a smoother soup, allow it to cool a little before blending.

Speedy Houmous (serves five)

You will need...

1 tin of chickpeas (drain it!);
1 lemon, juiced;
1 tablespoon of olive oil;
1 tablespoon of tahini paste.

Method

Use a blender to combine all of your ingredients in a bowl. Add some of the water from the chickpea can if the mixture seems too dry, and keep adding until you have a smooth, creamy paste. Serve with carrot sticks, cucumber and strips of pitta bread.

Real Chicken Nuggets (serves five)

You will need...

2 or 3 chicken breasts (skinless);
Fine breadcrumbs (from 2 slices of wholemeal bread);
Sunflower oil;
1 egg – blended;
3 or 4 tablespoons of plain flour – seasoned with salt and pepper.

Method

Cut the chicken breasts into strips or chunks. Roll these pieces in flour, then dip it in the egg. Put the chicken pieces into the breadcrumbs and ensure they get an even coating. Shallow-fry the breaded chicken until golden and cooked through, and remove the excess grease with kitchen paper. Put the "nuggests" in wraps with coleslaw as an alternative. Serve them with coleslaw, boiled potatoes, rice or a side salad.

Fasta Pasta Sauce

This sauce tastes better than the sauce you'll buy in supermarkets, costs less than half as much and is lower in fat and other nasties.

You will need...

1 tin of peeled plum tomatoes;
Sunflower or rapeseed oil;
Basil, salt & pepper;
1 clove garlic.

Method

Crush or chop the garlic and fry in the oil in a saucepan for a minute, very gently. Add the seasoning and tomatoes. Don't blend the tomatoes – instead, use a potato masher or fork to break them up. Simmer the sauce for 20 minutes, and mash it again until it's smooth but not runny.

For Bolognese, chop & add 1 onion, carrot & stick of celery at the beginning and 250g minced beef after the veg has browned. Add the sauce and some beef or vegetable stock, and simmer for 30 minutes.

If you want tuna pasta, add a can of drained tuna when the sauce is ready and mix it in.

What Have We Learned?

- Before you go grocery shopping, come up with a week's worth of snack and meal plans.
- Nobody is born a fussy eater. If you don't allow your child to be fussy, they'll learn not to be.
- Don't give up, a minor change is better than nothing.
- Master a few simple and easy recipes.

8

Building an Active Lifestyle

Experts agree that healthy eating alone is not enough to control weight or build up fitness - your child needs to be active! For children and young people, keeping active is the key to a healthy future, but it's also important for everyone else no matter their shape, weight or age.

Getting Active, Staying Active

In 2004 the British Heart Foundation produced "Couch Kids", a study into children's lifestyles. This study found active children to be less likely to smoke or use illegal drugs than children who are inactive, and more likely to study well and be successful in school. Building an active lifestyle will make it easier for your child to…

- Develop strong bones and grow up big and strong;
- Stay on top of medical issues like asthma;
- Reduce cholesterol and high blood pressure, lowering the risk of heart disease;
- Develop healthy exercise habits which they can carry into adulthood and pass on to their own children;
- De-stress, get rid of pent-up energy and sleep well;
- Achieve good self-esteem through setting goals and beating personal bests;
- Reach a good "energy balance" by burning excess calories and increasing metabolic rate;
- Have healthy heart and lung functions.

An active lifestyle produces more benefits than we could possibly hope to list here.

The Couch Kids study was repeated in 2009, and found that the recommended levels of physical activity (one hour per day) still were not being met by a significant proportion of young people, especially adolescent girls. In England, 19% of girls and 15% of boys weren't even getting 30 minutes of activity per day.

Are We Active?

With high percentages of children hitting the 60 minutes a day target, the British Heart Foundation's surveys did actually find a relatively positive picture of activity and fitness in the UK's young people and children.

The fizzy drinks and energy overloaded snacks that children now consume, however, mean that these positive figures still won't be enough to keep our kids healthy. Although 60 minutes is the recommended daily requirement, it is only a minimum and may not be enough for some children. Increasing activity *and* cutting out certain types of foods is the only way to effectively tackle obesity, and this is just further proof.

A big factor, according to the 2009 follow-up study, is parents' attitudes toward lifestyle and exercise. Parental denial was a major issue, and some parents simply don't understand what is enough activity and what is too little.

Child's Eye View

Children are more positive about exercise and keeping fit than they are about healthy eating, and they value sport and activity as a means of having a good time, meeting friends and keeping healthy. Research has suggested that many children are far more aware of healthy and unhealthy activities than most people would imagine, however tempting it is to blame their inactivity on too much TV.

Who Is at Risk?

The two Couch Kids studies identified a number of groups of children who were less likely to reach the recommended minimum amount of exercise than their peers. Children from less well off backgrounds fell into this bracket, and adolescent girls were also unlikely to reach their 60 minutes a day.

Despite being more likely to be overweight or obese, children from Afro Caribbean, South Asian and other ethnic minority backgrounds also tended to be less active than their counterparts in the white community.

What's the Problem?

In theory, it should be easy to get kids fired up and ready to go if they're as keen on activity and exercise as they say they are. So what's stopping them?

- Parents may not help their children to get involved if they're not leading active lives themselves;

- Non-sporty types will switch off if only competitive, selective team games are available. More suitable activities should be available;

- Busy family lives and other time constraints may stop parents from allowing their children to get involved in activities;

- Lack of time or other options - children have lots of exciting options to choose from now, or simply don't have the time;

- Lack of safe places to play locally - children and parents may feel strangers, older children and traffic pose too much of a risk.

Despite being more likely to be overweight or obese, children from Afro Caribbean, South Asian and other ethnic minority backgrounds also tended to be less active than their counterparts in the white community.

What Can Other Organisations Do to Help?

Speak to your child's school to see if there are any more activities they could get involved in. You should also see what's available for children in your local leisure or community centre. Organisations like Sport England, Sport Scotland, Sport Northern Ireland and the Sports Council for Wales are worth investigating as they should have advice and information on any special activities for children in your area.

Your child comes into contact with a lot of different organisations each week, and it's worth looking into what these groups might be able to do. Find out if your secondary school has any good lunchtime clubs running, or if your primary school encourages students to be active at break times.

If your child has a babysitter, visits relatives or spends time in day care, let them know that you're trying to keep them active and ask if they can help.

How Can I Help?

Encourage your child not to spend so much time in front of the television or the computer, and get involved together in regular weekend activities. For children trying to control their weight, it's not what you do but what you don't do that's important. You need to set a good example for your children by keeping active yourself. It's important that you support and show enthusiasm for your child's involvement in healthy activities. If you only visit one website, it should be Change4Life. Designed for adults and children, the Change4Life programme (**www.nhs.uk/change4life**) is a great way to get yourself more active. Their website is packed with suggestions, guidance, recipes, tips and downloads, all free of charge.

How Can We Build Up to 60 Minutes a Day?

At least 60 minutes of "moderate intensity" activity a day is necessary for a child to have a healthy lifestyle, according to government guidelines. It doesn't have to be done in one go and the activities your child can do to build up to the full 60 minutes can be varied - playing in the park, walking, scooting, bouncing on a trampoline, dancing or skipping - the list is endless. Playground games, swimming or cycling can all feed into this. You might need to aim for more, however, as this is just a minimum number.

Go Easy on the TV Time

Although children need down time, you should try to negotiate a reduction in viewing hours. With wall-to-wall children's channels and such a wide choice, it's no real surprise that an estimated 28% of UK children watch TV for more than four hours each day. One survey by OfCom found that 96% of 3-4 year olds watched 15 hours of TV on a television set, with an additional 41% also watching TV on other gadgets.

Many honest parents will admit that TV time is valuable to them as it lets them get their own things done while keeping the children quiet. In these cases, parents may add towards their children's 60 minutes a day by swapping 30 minutes of TV for something more active.

Choosing the Right Kind of Activity for Your Child

Even if you just go for a brisk walk around the park to start with, it's something to build on. When it comes to exercise and activity, you need to be very sensitive to what your child feels comfortable with (just as you need to be tactful when talking to your child about anything related to weight and obesity). Many people find swimming to be a great and highly enjoyable form of exercise but if your child has issues with their body image, it may be best to choose something else. Your best move is to begin with baby steps that your child can build on themselves. Consider activities like…

- Badminton;
- Climbing;
- Cycling;
- Dance mat;
- Football kick about;
- Frisbee;
- Games in the garden;
- Hike;
- Hula-hoop;
- Ice skating;
- Rollerblading;

- Scooting;
- Skating;
- Skipping;
- Swimming;
- Tennis;
- Trampoline;
- Walking;
- Walking the dog.

Make sure you have some indoor activities as well as outdoor ones so that you have things to do all year round.

See if your child would like to join a class, for example judo or martial arts, so they can do an activity on a regular basis. Make sure you have some indoor activities as well as outdoor ones so that you have things to do all year round.

The Easy Way to Fit In the Exercise

It's interesting that obesity rates have been rising as long as walking to school has been decreasing. Walking to school and back has many benefits. Leaving the car at home is an easy way to help your child reach their 60 minutes a day. If there are compelling reasons for you to drive, see if there is a "walking bus" for your child to join or park away from the school and let your child walk the last few minutes.

- Around 8-14 minutes of your child's activity each day could be made up by the average walk to and/or from school.
- Over a week of walking to and from school, a child aged 12-13 will burn more calories than they would in a two-hour PE class.
- Children who walk to school are more likely to play sport.
- Boys who walk to school are more active after school and in the evening compared to those who travel by car.

Less congestion around the school makes the journey to school safer, so if as many people as possible could walk instead, everyone would be a winner.

More Tips for Reaching 60

- Get a pedometer! This will let your child beat personal bests, time and count their steps and do their own time trials. Many pedometers will also have a calorie counter to measure how much energy your child uses up.

- Make it fun! Keep things as relaxed and enjoyable as possible. Whether it's a game of cricket, a skipping game or a walk in the rain, you're not training for the Olympics so you may as well have some fun with it.

- Make it sociable! Activities are often better if more than one child joins in, whether that's a sibling or a friend from school. Your child will find it much easier to stay enthusiastic and motivated.

- Celebrate achievements! Aim to build up to other more exciting activities, or buy your child small gifts like new trainers or a football. Make sure you recognise and congratulate your child on their achievements.

- If you're comfortable with your child being out in the neighbourhood, send them round the block on a scooter or bike.

- Try to build physical activity into your everyday family life. Walk when you can, play games in the garden or visit the park on your way home from school.

- Aim to make smooth progress, letting your child control the pace. Try to introduce challenging new activities and keep pushing the boundaries to get a sense of achievement.

What Have We Learned?

- Your child's health now and in the future can be improved if you get active today.
- Step away from the screen and leave the car at home.
- Be sensitive to your child's feelings about activity, exercise and sport.
- Remove barriers that may be stopping your child from getting active.

9

Reaching the Finish Line

Getting Special Help

You might want to think about getting in touch with some specialists who can help you if you've already tried to lose weight without support and have had little or no success. This doesn't mean that someone else is going to take over responsibility for your child - you will still need to be as involved and supportive as before, but there are many advantages to using expert support:

- Some children just respond better to advice from people they aren't related to.
- Support will be available to both you and your child.
- Your child is likely to be more committed to their goals.
- The advice you get will be up-to-date and appropriate

This can also come in handy if you're just not feeling confident in your ability to give your child the advice and guidance they need.

Sourcing Your Options

From obesity clinics to special residential holidays and camps, the size of the UK's obesity problem means that there are plenty of healthcare professionals who focus on this area and provide many different options for children. Every area has its own schemes and projects, however, as there's no regional or national UK standard for treating obesity.

What's available in your area and how you go about enrolling your child at a clinic or club depends on what sort of services are provided and paid for in your health board area. Projects seem to be more concentrated in major cities, and the type of support that's available to you and your child strongly hinges on where you live.

To find out what options are available to you, talk to your GP or healthcare team before bringing these suggestions to your child.

What Does Success Look Like?

There are loads of good things to look forward to. While we've mostly focussed on the terrible things that can happen to children who are overweight or obese, the future can still be bright. Your child will be able to enjoy many benefits if they get active and adopt a healthy diet. For example, you may find they…

- Run about better and get more enjoyment from sports;
- Have fewer issues with their skin, hair and teeth;
- Find it easier to control health conditions like asthma;
- Fit more comfortably in clothes for their own age group;
- Have a better understanding of nutrition and healthy eating;
- Be more confident and comfortable with their body shape;
- Be protected from bad diseases in adulthood;
- Play more energetic games with friends;
- Not get out of breath or puff and pant;
- Concentrate more at school.

Establishing healthy eating and activity patterns that will last a lifetime is the goal here, not just embarking on a weight control stint. It's important that your child understands this and knows the difference.

Better Self-Esteem

A child lacking in confidence, or whose family are experiencing problems, may turn to food for comfort. This becomes a self-defeating vicious circle, as overeating and weight gain will cause a further loss of self-esteem and isolation. Increased self-confidence is one of the great benefits that many parents find their children have gained after embarking on weight control and increased activity.

Many children will overeat for a wide range of reasons - while we've talked about the "obesogenic environment" and a lack of exercise, these aren't the only causes. Unwanted weight gain and comfort eating can easily stem from feelings of loneliness, stress and inadequacy. If it's a response to bullying or problems at home, these will need to be addressed as part of the overall picture. It's important to look at patterns and figure out reasons why a child might be overeating.

Some children may benefit from getting involved in a formal group, as meeting others in the same boat and seeing how they tackle obesity can act as an incentive. Feelings of strength and confidence are attained by many children when they tackle their condition and discover that they can make positive changes to their own lives.

Unwanted weight gain and comfort eating can easily stem from feelings of loneliness, stress and inadequacy.

How Long Is This Going to Take?

Making lifestyle changes is very hard - but once you decide to leave the car at home and walk to school, you will need to stick to it. You will be setting off on a healthy eating and activity programme that lasts a lifetime, so there won't be any stage at which you'll stop and return to old habits. The road to a healthier lifestyle will take as long as it takes, and that's different for everyone.

Use a food diary or activity plan for as long as they are useful to your child, but don't labour them if the novelty is wearing off. The diary might come in handy if you or your child begin slipping back into old habits. Explain to your child that you aren't banning anything, just cutting back and substituting, as they may well be upset by the concept of losing their favourite snacks and treats forever.

Help them to understand that there are going to be some new approaches to food and activity, but they can still have their favourite treats every now and then. Until the good eating and activity habits take hold and become a normal part of everyday life, you'll need to work hard to keep your child as motivated as you can.

A child will find it very de-motivating if they think you are disappointed. Value every step your child takes towards becoming healthier, and try to keep your own goals and expectations as achievable as possible.

Changes that Last a Lifetime

Try to get your child to think of themselves as a pioneer or trendsetter and see if you can get family and friends to follow suit. In the same way as giving up smoking or becoming a vegetarian, adopting a healthy lifestyle is not something that can be reversed. It's really important to make sure your child understands that this isn't a temporary thing, this is the plan from now on. You and your child will need to be entirely committed, as there are no half-measures when it comes to lifelong health. Your child can't just be "a bit healthy" or "healthy every second day".

Giving Up and Slipping Up

It would be very unusual for a child to drop all their old inactive habits and not get cravings for certain foods. Your child is likely to give up or slip up once or twice along the way, and you need to be prepared for this. A few detours from the main path shouldn't make such a big difference, so long as you've come to an understanding about what you're doing and why, and they're on board with the general plan.

Checking Expectations

People will be sizing your child up and looking for changes. Some sort of radical transformation may well be expected by your child and their friends, and it makes sense that they'll expect their drastic changes to have drastic results. A solution to this could be to make sure that your child does change week on week by getting a new haircut or new items of clothing. This can take some attention away from losing weight, as there will be different visible changes for people to focus on.

If there's pressure from friends and family to see results and you and your child are taking things slowly, it can be very frustrating for your child. After all, children aren't really known for their patience.

Rewarding Positive Behaviour

What you're doing is in your child's best interests, and it's important that they understand that. Try to back up this understanding by…

- Congratulating your child for making good choices.
- Telling them stories about times they've done things successfully.
- Showing them you have confidence in them.
- Keeping the positive encouragement going.

Older children could be given a weekly "surprise" for doing well in the form of a small present, music or game download, stationary, favourite toy, anything that is non-food. Tracking progress through start chart systems are especially helpful for younger children.

Keeping a Child Motivated and Optimistic

- Make sure your child remembers their goals and their reasons for making these changes.
- Try to introduce some variety into your child's daily activities to keep them interested.
- Remind them of things they did really well and can do again.
- Keep on with the healthy eating but try to vary it a bit if the menu is getting boring.

It's helpful if you can be positive about what you're doing so your child doesn't see this as an exercise in being deprived of their favourite things. Arranging things like visits to people who have been successful in similar endeavours, new activities and family outings is a great way to keep things interesting. Your child is likely to carry on if you're able to invent ways to keep them on track and make sure the whole family is behind them. This is why family support is so vital.

Make sure your child notices how much more energy they have now, or how much healthier they look.

Only You Can Help Your Child

You will have helped teach your child to do many things in life such as getting dressed, crossing the road, learning to read or riding a bike. Your child will be depending on you to make sure that they aren't among the 50% of children who are predicted to be obese by 2050. The obesity time bomb, at the end of the day, will only be beaten if parents put in the effort to help their children. This is a lot more serious than the other things you'll need to help them with, but the steps you need to take aren't all that different.

What Have We Learned?

- Keep your child on track, and make sure they stay positive and motivated.
- Your child's achievements need to be recognised and reinforced.
- Parents are the best people to help their child beat obesity.
- Be prepared for slipping back to bad habits.

Help List

Where Can I Learn More?

What help is available will vary according to where you live. The latest information and contacts will be available from your doctor's surgery or local hospital, which should be your first port of call if you're thinking of making changes to your child's lifestyle. This is particularly important if your child has any other medical conditions.

You should also ask your local pharmacist for advice and information, or contact your child's school and see if the nurse can offer any support. Nobody will know as much about your child's health as your health visitor, practice nurse or family doctor, so it's really important that you speak to one of these members of your local healthcare team. The options open to your child can be explained and recommended to you by your healthcare team.

Get together with other parents to organise an activity - it could be basketball, judo, cheerleading, aerobics or anything your child would like. Try your local leisure centre to find out about fitness activities. They could have special schemes, courses or reduced prices for young people. Children trying to control their weight may be targeted by some of their special facilities, and it's worth finding out about this.

If you find something you think would help your child, let them see it but don't insist if they are not interested. Clubs for children and other special activities are often available in local community centres. You could even start a class of your own if you don't see anything suitable for your child.

While you'll need to be selective and work out which sites are more useful than others, the internet is generally a fantastic place to find all sorts of useful information. Children and young people may well be able to find websites designed specially for people like them.

The following list will be a good starting point, though there are way too many organisations focussed on child obesity and wellbeing to try and list here.

Weight-Loss Surgery Information

British Obesity Surgery Patient Association
www.bospa.org
Tel: 08456 02 04 46
BOSPA (British Obesity Surgery Patients Association) was launched in December 2003 to provide support and information to the thousands of patients in the UK for whom obesity surgery can provide an enormous benefiTel:

Weight Loss Surgery Information and Support
www.wlsinfo.org.uk
Tel: 0151 222 4737
WLSinfo, 54 St James Street, Liverpool L1 0AB
Although this site is geared to adults, you can use it to access information and advice about children and to learn about what is involved in weight loss surgery. WLSinfo is a registered charity set up and run entirely by volunteers and maintained by donations from members. They are a leading source of support and guidance around weight loss surgery options in the UK.

Resources for Schools and Teachers

The Caroline Walker Trust

www.cwt.org.uk

Tel: 01923 445374

22 Kindersley Way, Abbots Langley, Herts, WD5 0DQ

The charity produced guidelines, training materials and expert information on child nutrition needs in school and also on special needs nutrition. This organisation aims to help members of vulnerable groups who need assistance with nutrition and food. Their guidance is invaluable to anyone who cares for children.

Food Dudes (Ireland)

www.fooddudes.ie/main.html

Tel: 01 522 4855

Email: fooddudes@realnation.ie

Real Nation, 24 Arran Quay, Dublin 7, Ireland.

Food Dudes is a programme developed by the University of Wales, Bangor, to encourage children to eat more fruit and vegetables both in school and at home. In large-scale studies in schools in England and Wales and pilot studies in schools in Ireland, the Programme has been shown to be effective and results long lasting across the primary age range.

Association for the Study of Obesity (ASO)

www.aso.org.uk

Tel: 07847 2438309 (Office Hours: Tuesday to Thursday, 9.30am to 2.30pm)

Email: ASOoffice@aso.org.uk

ASO, PO Box 5413, Brighton BN50 8HH

Dedicated to the understanding and treatment of obesity, this organisation was first set up in 1967. Although the site is not aimed at parents, there is good advice, useful links and contacts. They aim to spread awareness of obesity and the impacts it can have on a person's health, as well as promote the prevention and treatment of the condition and research and understand its causes. The site also has some handy videos and information to use in the classroom.

Exercise, Activity and Sporting Information

National Sports Agencies

These organisations are responsible for promoting sport and active lifestyles in their respective areas. They encourage people at all levels to get more involved in physical activity and are a good source of information if you are looking for advice about special activities and initiatives for children where you live.

Scotland: sportscotland

www.sportscotland.org.uk
Tel: 0141 534 6500
Email: sportscotland.enquiries@sportscotland.org.uk
Doges, Templeton on the Green, 62 Templeton Street, Glasgow G40 1DA

England: Sport England

www.sportengland.org
Tel: 0345 8508 508
Email: funding@sportengland.org
21 Bloomsbury Street, London, WC1B 3HF

Wales: Sport Wales

http://sport.wales/
Tel: 0300 300 3111
F. 0300 300 3108
Email: info@sportwales.org.uk
Sport Wales, Sophia Gardens, Cardiff CF11 9SF

Northern Ireland: Sport NI

www.sportni.net
Tel: 028 9038 1222
Email: info@sportni.net
2a Upper Malone Road, Belfast BT9 5LA

Food

British Nutrition Foundation
www.nutrition.org.uk
Tel: 020 7557 7930
Email: postbox@nutrition.org.uk
New Derwent House, 69-73 Theobalds Road, London WC1X 8TA
The British Nutrition Foundation provides healthy eating information, resources for schools, news items, recipes and details of the work going on around the UK. The website has lots of information on food and activities and includes special sections for children.

The Eatwell Guide
www.nhs.uk/live-well/eat-well/the-eatwell-guide/
This website is full of advice to help you eat more healthily. There's an excellent Eatwell plate like the one featured in this book and recipes which help you work out exactly what you're eating. More information is available from the Food Standards Agency.

www.food.gov.uk
General: Email: helpline@food.gov.uk
Tel: 020 7276 8829
Wales: Email: walesadminteam@food.gov.uk
Tel: 029 2067 8999
Northern Ireland: Email: infofsani@food.gov.uk
Tel: 028 9041 7700

Food and Drink Federation (FDF)
www.fdf.org.uk
Tel: 020 7836 2460
F. 020 7836 0580
6th Floor, 10 Bloomsbury Way, London WC1A 2SL
The Food and Drink Federation (FDF) is the voice of the UK food and drink industry, the largest manufacturing sector in the country.

The Food Commission

www.foodcomm.org.uk

Tel: 020 7837 2250

Email: enquiries@foodcomm.org.uk

94 White Lion Street, London N1 9PF

The Food Commission campaigns for the right for everyone to eat safe, wholesome, good quality food. It has also developed a website designed for independent use by secondary school students aged 11-14 or for anyone who is interested in how our food is produced and what its effect is on our health and the environmenTel:

Weight Wise Website - British Dietetic Association

www.bdaweightwise.com

This is an independent site with unbiased, easy-to-follow hints and tips based on the latest evidence to help you manage weight for good. It will help you take a look at your child's current eating habits and physical activity levels, and offer a practical approach to setting goals for a lifestyle change.

NHS Sites for Different Areas of the UK

These are useful gateway sites to access in depth information and support relevant to the area where you live. Scotland, Northern Ireland, England and Wales all have different NHS sites, which you can find below. Through these you will be able to find information about what's going on in your local area. Available treatments as well as information on healthy living, children's health and medical facts about the causes of obesity can be found on each website.

England: www.nhs.uk
Northern Ireland: http://online.hscni.net/
Scotland: www.show.scot.nhs.uk
Wales: www.wales.nhs.uk

Healthcare Improvement Scotland (NHS QIS)
www.nhshealthquality.org
General queries and feedback: comments.his@nhs.net
Tel: 0131 623 4300
Edinburgh office: Gyle Square, 1 South Gyle Crescent, Edinburgh EH12 9EB
Glasgow office: Delta House, 50 West Nile Street, Glasgow G1 2NP
Set up to improve quality of care and treatment delivered by NHS Scotland.

General Information

BANT – British Association for Nutrition and Lifestyle Medicine
www.bant.org.uk
Email: theadministrator@bant.org.uk
Tel: 0870 606 1284
BANT, 27 Old Gloucester Street, London WC1N 3XX
The primary function of BANT is to assist its members in attaining the highest standards of integrity, knowledge, competence and professional practice, in order to protect the client's interests, nutritional therapy and the Nutritional Therapist.

British Association for Counselling and Psychotherapy
www.bacp.co.uk
Email: bacp@bacp.co.uk
Tel: 01455 883300
Twitter: @BACP
BACP, 15 St John's Business Park, Lutterworth, Leicestershire LE17 4HB, United Kingdom
This professional association advises schools on setting up counselling services, assists the NHS on service provision, works with voluntary agencies and supports independent practitioners. Find a therapist on their website.

Clare Jones – Nutritional Therapy
www.clarejones-nutrition.co.uk
Tel: 07985 166606
Email: info@clarejones-nutrition.co.uk
Works with clients to produce, for each, an individually tailored programme, including dietary changes, supplements and lifestyle advice.

Coeliac UK
www.coeliac.org.uk
Tel: 0333 332 2033
Provides expert and independent information to help people manage their health and dieTel:

Department of Health and Social Care

https://www.gov.uk/government/organisations/department-of-health-and-social-care

Address: Ministerial Correspondence and Public Enquiries Unit, Department of Health and Social Care, 39 Victoria Street, London SW1H 0EU, United Kingdom

Tel: 0207 210 4850

Supports ministers in leading the nation's health and social care to help people live more independent, healthier lives for longer.

Department of Health for Northern Ireland

www.health-ni.gov.uk

Address: Department of Health, Information Office, C5.20, Castle Buildings, Stormont, Belfast, Northern Ireland BT4 3SQ

Tel: 028 9052 0500

Email: webmaster@health-ni.gov.uk

Provides information on health, social services and safety in Northern Ireland. Visit the publications section for more information.

Family Action

www.family-action.org.uk

Address: Family Action Head Office, 24 Angel Gate, City Road, London EC1V 2PT

Tel: 020 7254 6251

Email: info@family-action.org.uk

Family Action works to tackle some of the most complex and difficult issues facing families today – including financial hardship, mental health problems, social isolation, learning disabilities, domestic abuse, or substance misuse and alcohol problems.

Family Lives

http://familylives.org.uk/

Family Lives Head Office: 020 7553 3080

15-17 The Broadway, Hatfield, Hertfordshire, AL9 5HZ

Trained family support workers, both paid and volunteer, offer all family members immediate and ongoing help on the phone, online or in local communities.

GOV.UK

www.gov.uk

The best place to find government services and information – Simpler, clearer, faster.

Healthy Start
www.healthystart.nhs.uk

This website is specially geared to families on benefits and offers advice on where to use food and milk vouchers and how to make sure children are getting a healthy dieTel:

Inspire
www.inspirewellbeing.org

Email: NI/UK: hello@inspirewellbeing.org

Ireland: dundalk@inspirewellbeing.ie

Tel: 028 9032 8474

Address NI/UK: Inspire Central Office, Lombard House, 10-20 Lombard Street, Belfast BT1 1RD

Ireland: Inspire Dundalk Office, Clontygora Drive, Muirhevnamor, Dundalk, Co.Louth

A range of services for people with mental health needs. Has 14 Beacon Centres across Northern Ireland providing support, social activities, outreach, alternative therapies, education and discussions.

Mental Health Foundation
www.mentalhealth.org.uk

London office (headquarters): Colechurch House, 1 London Bridge Walk, London, SE1 2SX

Tel: +44 (0)20 7803 1100

Glasgow office: Merchants House, 30 George Square, Glasgow, G2 1EG

Tel: +44 (0)141 572 0125

Cardiff office: Castle Court, 6 Cathedral Road, Cardiff, CF11 9LJ

Tel: +44 (0)2921 679 400

UK's charity for everyone's mental health. Aims to find and address the sources of mental health problems.

The MEND Programme
www.mytimeactive.co.uk/cwm

Tel: 020 8328 1777

Linden House, 153-155 Masons Hill, Bromley BR2 9HY

An organisation that improves the wellbeing of its customers and their communities through well-manages, accessible and good value leisure, gold and health services.

Mind, the Mental Health Charity
www.mind.org.uk
Address: 15-19 Broadway, Stratford, London E15 4BQ
Tel: 020 8519 2122
Email: supporterrelations@mind.org.uk
Mind Cymru: 3rd Floor, Castlebridge 4, Castlebridge, 5-19 Cowbridge Road East,
Cardiff CF11 9AB
Tel: 029 2039 5123
Email: supporterrelations@mind.org.uk
There are around 200 local MIND associations in England and Wales. Search for your local branch onsite. MIND campaigns for equal rights and challenges discrimination and other services for those with mental health needs. The website includes lots of information and free factsheets.

MoreLife
https://more-life.co.uk/
Tel: 0113 812 5233
F. 0844 209 0884
Email: team@more-life.co.uk
An organisation that provides programmes and services to individuals that will help them change their behaviours and make a difference to their overall health and wellbeing.

National Obesity Forum
www.nationalobesityforum.org.uk
Email: nof@omniamed.com
Established by health professionals in May 2000 to raise awareness of the growing impact that obesity was having. One of the most high-profile organisations involved in obesity campaigning. A very comprehensive site and a good source of up-to-date information on nutrition and exercise for children, and where to get help.

NHS Change4Life
www.nhs.uk/change4life
Change4Life is a big government campaign running in England and Wales but anyone can use the website and it has links to similar schemes in other parts of the UK. The site is packed with everything you'll need (except the willpower!) to get fit and healthy. It can even generate a free personalised action plan in response to a few questions.

Patient

https://patient.info/

Patient empowers everyone to take charge of their health. Their trusted clinical information, written and reviewed by an extensive network of doctors and healthcare professionals, helps people to feel better and live longer.

Patrick Holford

www.patrickholford.com

Tel: 0370 334 1575

Address: 14 St John's Road, Tunbridge Wells, Kent TN4 9NP

Provides you with trusted and credible information on key issues about your health and nutrition written by Patrick Holford and other leading experts.

Weight Concern

www.weightconcern.org.uk

Email: equiries@weightconcern.org.uk

Tel: 020 7679 1853

F. 020 7679 8354

Weight Concern, 1-19 Torrington Place, London WC1E 7HB

A UK charity committed to developing and researching new treatments for weight issues and obesity and supporting self-help. No helpline or individual advice is offered but the website is very detailed, includes a children's BMI calculator and has lots of child specific information.

Weight Loss Resources

www.weightlossresources.co.uk

Weight Loss Resources provides calorie and nutritional information. It gives you all the facts on what your body needs, and provides all the tools you need to take control, lose weight and eat well. A calorie counter and exercise diary is included.

TakeLifeOn.co.uk (Scotland)

www.takelifeon.co.uk

Giving you practical steps to healthier eating and being active, this website offers practical advice on making small but important lifestyle changes.

Resources for Black & Minority Ethnic Groups

DASH/DEAL

http://dash.sphsu.mrc.ac.uk/

Of interest to everyone but of special interest to ethnic minority groups - the Medical Research Council (MRS) funded project is looking into how the authorities can enhance healthy living amongst secondary school aged children from diverse backgrounds. Lots of information for parents, teachers and researchers.

South Asian Health Foundation

http://www.sahf.org.uk

Email: sahfsecretariat@gmail.com

Tel: 07807 069719

39 Westfield Road, Edgbaston, Birmingham, West Midlands B15 3QE

A UK based charity aiming to promote health & further research into health issues involving people of South Asian origin. The site contains useful information contacts and links.

Information on Parenting

Netmums

www.netmums.com

Email: contactus@netmums.com

Henry Wood House, 2 Riding House Street, London W1W 7FA

Netmums is a local UK network for mums (and dads), offering a wealth of information on both a national and local level. You can access local support information and swap advice with other parents. Lots of good articles about healthy eating and food.

Health and Children's Charity Organisations

The health charities listed below are involved in conditions that healthy children really don't need to be suffering from. Most have offices based in Wales, Northern Ireland and Scotland and some have offices in regions of England. They all have useful information for parents, carers and professionals relating to their specialist area. Because of the scale of the problem and what it will mean for children's future health, each of these groups takes an active interest in the issue of child obesity. Useful contacts, links and eating and activity guides can also be found through some of their websites.

Barnardos
www.barnardos.org.uk
Tel: 020 8550 8822
Tanners Lane, Barkingside, Ilford, Essex, IG6 1QG

British Heart Foundation
www.bhf.org.uk
Tel: 0300 330 3322
Email: heretohelp@bhf.org.uk
Text: 18001 0300 330 3322
British Heart Foundation, Lyndon Place, 2096 Coventry Road, Sheldon, Birmingham B26 3YU

Cancer Research UK
www.cancerresearch.org.uk
Tel: (General Enquiries) 0300 123 1022 – Monday to Friday, 8am to 6pm
Cancer Questions: 0808 800 4040
Cancer Research UK, PO BOX 1561, Oxford OX4 9GZ

Diabetes UK
www.diabetes.org.uk
Tel: 0345 123 2399
F. 020 7424 1001
Email: helpline@diabetes.org.uk
Diabetes UK Central Office, Wells Lawrence House, 126 Back Church Lane, London E1 1FH

Resources Around the World

Alliance for a Healthier Generation
www.healthiergeneration.org

Supported by former US President Bill Clinton and Governor of California Arnold Schwarzenegger, the Alliance aims to prevent childhood obesity and create healthier lifestyles for all children. Healthcare professionals, parents and teachers can all find helpful information on this US-based website.

American Heart Association
www.heart.org

This site contains some great information about healthy eating and smart lifestyle choices.

World Health Organisation
www.who.int/topics/obesity/en/

The World Health Organisation is the directing and coordinating authority on international health within the United Nations' system. Lots of information and help from a global perspective. Their website has a special section that deals with obesity at an international level, and is great for things like technical figures and information.

When it comes to encouraging a child to bring about changes in lifestyle patterns, one source will be more important than any of the other resources and connections you can find. You have the potential to help your child change their life for the better and to grow up and develop as a happier and more confident person. Details and information are very important and helpful, but none of it will help if a child doesn't have their family's supporTel: All of the other difficulties they'll have to face in life can be tackled with greater enthusiasm and courage when your child knows that they have a healthy future assured, and while the journey will be tough the results will be more than worth iTel:

Sources

Cunningham, Solveig A. et al. "Incidence of Childhood Obesity in the United States." *The New England Journal of Medicine* (January 2014).

Effects of childhood asthma on the development of obesity among school-aged children, Zhanghua Chen et al., *American Journal of Respiratory and Critical Care*, doi: abs/10.1164/rccm.201608-1691OC, published online 19 January 2017, abstract.

University of Colorado Cancer Center. "Long-term effects of childhood obesity on late-life health revealed by study." *ScienceDaily*, 12 February 2014.
www.sciencedaily.com/releases/2014/02/140212132629.htm

British Heart Foundation. "Couch Kids: the nation's future…", 2009.
http://www.ssehsactive.org.uk/userfiles/Documents/NewCouchKids1.pdf